For Such a Time as This
A Cookbook

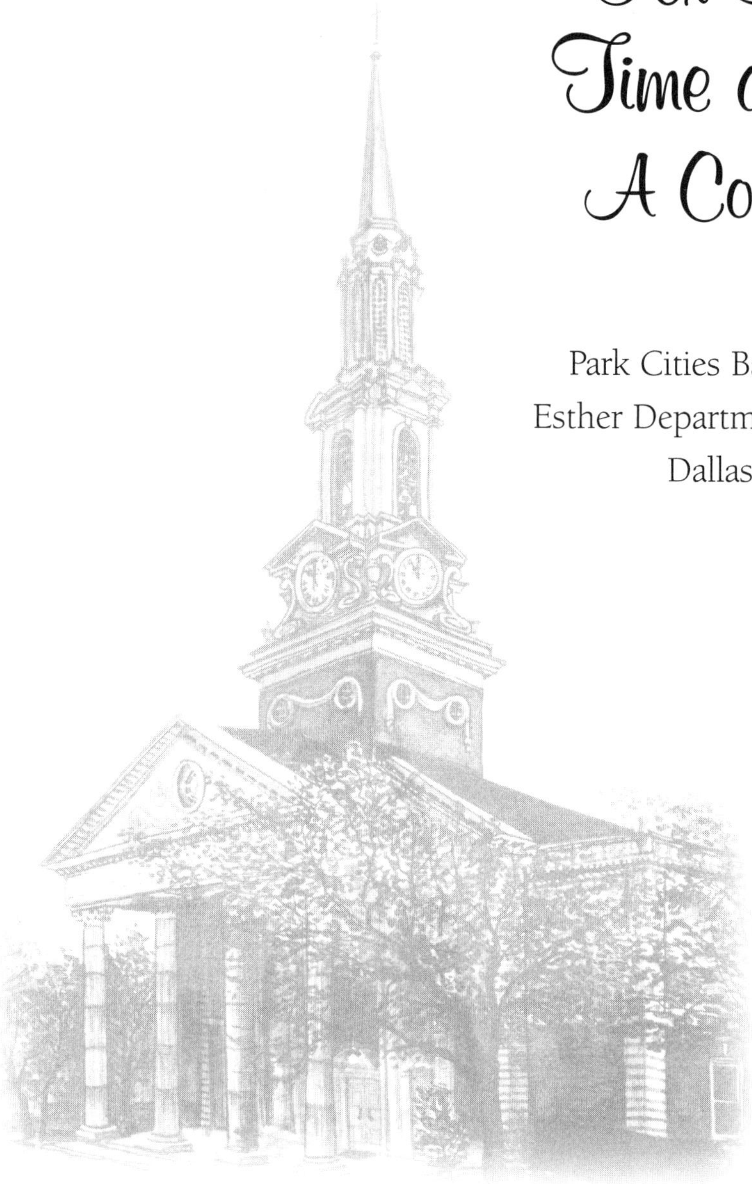

Park Cities Baptist Church
Esther Department and Friends
Dallas, Texas

For Such a Time as This
A Cookbook

Published by Park Cities Baptist Church
Esther Department and Friends

3933 Northwest Parkway
Dallas, Texas 75225
214-860-1500
www.pcbc.org

This cookbook is a collection of favorite recipes,
which are not necessarily original recipes.

ISBN: 0-9740527-0-1

Edited, Designed, and Manufactured by

CommunityClassics™
An imprint of

FRP

P.O. Box 305142
Nashville, Tennessee 37230
800-358-0560

Manufactured in the United States of America
First Printing: 2003
Number of copies: 3,000

Contents

Cookbook Committee

Lisa Anderson
Beth Grace
Cookbook Committee Co-Chairs

Suzanna Reed
Cover Design

Dorthy Miller Shore
Creative Design and Layout

Linda Alexander
Laurie Ewing
Valerie Morgan
Recipe Testing and Menu Selection

Suzanne Griffin
Stacey Lake
Text

Candice Cowen
Typesetting

Carol Bayless
Proofreading

Brooksie Braden
Accounting and Finance

Deborah Ethridge Sutton
Legal Counsel

Mitzi Rudderow
Marketing and Sales

Stacie Harris
Support and Distribution

Janet Denison
Alice Fant
Department Leaders

Special Thanks

The cookbook committee gratefully
acknowledges the generous contributions of

Paul Skipworth for his professional expertise
and talent in photographing the cover

Dr. Jeff Warren, Pastor of First Baptist Church McKinney
and former staff member of Park Cities Baptist Church,
for his artistic rendering of the church

Suzan Holten for her drawing of the sanctuary
arches and *The Miller Agency* for its valuable assistance
with the creative design and layout

Contributors

Lane Aaberg
Karen Anderson
Claudette Ballard
Gayle Barnes
Emily Boyd
Barbara Brim
Margie Bruner
Susan Bussey
Patty Butcher
Carolyn Cardinal
Sarah Carter
Mary Lynn Chance
Ruth Clemmons
Fran Connell
Sheila Cook
Leila Cornelius
Whitney Cortner
Candis Couch
Frann Davis
Sally Davis
Katherine Davoust-Ayala
Karen Dollar
Stephanie Dowdall
Janda Edwards
Barbara Hunt Elkins
Debbie Evans
Vicki Farrow
Sara Foxworth
Mary Gill
Betty Greer
Sally Griffiths
Donna Hafner
Sheila Harris
Gloria Hart
Cathy Hawes
Kellye Hawes
Joan Henderson
Amy Hillman
Susan Hirschler
Stephanie Hogan
Cynthia Homer
Suzanne Humphreys
Janet Jelen
Christie Justice
Dottie Kingston
Elizabeth Kinslow
Pam Lane
Babs Lawrence

Denise Livingstone
Kathy Magee
Markay Marshall
Lou Mayfield
Shirley McCutchin
Kathy McDaniel
Suzanne McWhorter
Elizabeth Meadows
Rebecca Meadows
Vickie Meadows
Joan Melton
Karla Ness
Debi Newman
Kathy Nikolas
Betty Pelt
Teena Pennington
Bridget Person
Kyle Planas
Melinda Ramsey
Kimberly Raphael
Cyndi Reynolds
Brenda Richardson
Laura Riley
Susie Roberts
Betty Shaw
Janet Showers
Jann Skelton
Lisa Sims
Jaime Smith
Bet Stewart
Sheree Stephens
Julia Taylor
Traci Thomas
Kay Threadgill
Kelly Trabold
Mary Tucker
Katie Walker
Faith Weaver
Janis Wilber
Susan Williams
Libbie Wilmer
Andria Wisner
Nina Yee
Libby York
LaSonya Zackery
Peggy Zadina

Preface

Planting trees we'll not sit under

These words are my favorite definition of significance, and they capture the vision and legacy that is Park Cities Baptist Church.

In 1939, a handful of visionaries determined that "there ought to be a church in the Park Cities." Meeting without the sponsorship of any church, they began their own congregation in a schoolhouse. A home on Lovers Lane was their next stop, then a field on the far-north edge of Dallas. They had no way to know that their vision would grow into a congregation of over 9,000 members, with missions and ministries stretching around the world. But God did.

Now our congregation is "continuing the vision," extending our legacy into the future. This next chapter of our history will provide critical space for preschoolers, children, and youth. It will enable us to expand our ministry to our community. It will secure the future of our church as we reach the next generation for our Lord.

The book you hold in your hand is an important part of that future. The Esther Department has found a very creative way to help us fulfill God's vision for our congregation. The proceeds from this project will directly benefit the building campaign, thus ministering to generations of children and families to come. I am personally grateful to each of the ladies who have given so sacrificially of their time and abilities to make such a significant commitment to our future.

The Lord assures his people, *I know the plans I have for you, plans to prosper you and not to harm you, plans to give you hope and a future* (Jeremiah 29:11). His plans are greater than any we can conceive. No one in 1939 could have imagined our church in 2003. May we be as faithful to God's vision as those who have gone before us. Then we will help people follow Jesus, planting trees for generations to come. This is the promise of God.

PARK·CITIES
BAPTIST CHURCH

Jim Denison

Dr. James C. Denison
Senior Pastor

Introduction

And who knows but that you have come to royal position for such a time as this?
Esther 4:14

In the Old Testament, the book of Esther tells the story of a young queen faced with a difficult decision. A proclamation signed by her husband, the king, condemns all Jews to die. Knowing that he is unaware that she is a Jew, Esther risks death as she reveals her heritage and asks that the Jewish nation be saved. Strengthened by these words—and who knows but that you have come to royal position for such a time as this—Esther speaks to the king. He revokes his proclamation, and a nation survives. This story of a woman of great faith and unwavering desire to serve her Lord challenges each of us to follow her example in courage, faith, service, and love.

The Esther Department of Park Cities Baptist Church began meeting for Sunday School in January of 1999. United in Christ, women with diverse occupations, interests, gifts, and abilities gather each week to study God's word. In the writing and distribution of ***For Such a Time as This***, the Esther Department commits to continuing the vision of the members of Park Cities Baptist Church by doing its part to support the new Community Life Center, a place dedicated to helping people follow Jesus.

Eight beams support the sanctuary of Park Cities Baptist Church. Inscribed on each is a scripture verse of utmost importance to the Christian life. It is with these verses that each chapter of our cookbook begins, followed by a brief glimpse into the history and traditions of the women of the church. It is our hope that this cookbook will be a blessing not only to our church, but also to all who will enjoy the wonderful recipes lovingly gathered within these pages.

For Such a Time as This is a delectable collection of recipes that can be enjoyed individually or combined with others to make any party or holiday function a memorable experience. As you open this book and begin your culinary journey, experience the legacy we are so blessed to call Park Cities Baptist Church. Our prayer is that this book will be a blessing to your home, your family, and your table.

For such a time as this,
Esther Department and Friends

Serve the Lord with gladness:
come before his presence with singing.

Psalm 100:2

Park Cities Baptist Church has been blessed with a rich heritage of women who opened their homes and hearts to fellow church members and to the community. For many years, Thelma McCann hosted the end-of-the-year picnic for the Park Cities Baptist Church Women's Missionary Union, an organization dedicated to supporting missions throughout the world through prayer, service, and offerings. The women of the church appreciated the opportunity to travel to her country home at the corner of Rambler Road and Walnut Hill Lane for an afternoon of picking pecans and enjoying good food.

Faithfully, these ladies and so many more began a legacy of hospitality and service, serving the Lord with gladness.

Menus

A Little Romance

Blue Cheese Logs

Cornish Hens with Wild Rice

Strawberry Spinach Salad

Dinner Rolls

Coffee Royal Cake

Christmas Morning Memories

Cheddar Cheese Ring

Ham Balls

Cinnamon Candied Apples

Caramel French Toast or Sticky Buns

Charleston Cheese Grits

Orange Wassail

Autumn's Abundance

Poblano Corn Chowder

Stuffed Pork Tenderloin

Green Beans with Caramelized Onions

Sweet Potato Casserole

Fresh Spinach Salad or Field Greens and Crumbled Blue Cheese Salad

Elegant Layered Apple Cake or Pecan Pie Squares

A Plantation Easter

Apricot Glazed Pork Tenderloin

Asparagus Soufflé or Calabacitas (Squash Casserole)

Honey-Glazed Baby Carrots

Garden Salad with Almonds and Oranges

Herbed Rolls

Carrot Cake with Cream Cheese Frosting or Strawberry Cake

Delta Mint Tea

A Mid-Morning Mother's Tea

Savory Summer Pie or Crescent Sausage Roll

Cucumber Sandwiches or
Curried Chicken Tea Sandwiches

Congealed Orange Salad

Blueberry Coffee Cake or a Bread Tray
(Strawberry Nut Bread, Banana Bread,
Poppy Seed Muffins, Zucchini Nut Muffins)

Luscious Lemon Squares

Pineapple Tea or Almond Tea

A Great Christmas Celebration

Spinach Artichoke Dip or
Brie and Pear Quesadillas

Special Beef Tenderloin

Bibb Salad with Raspberry Maple Dressing

Cheese Potatoes or Roasted Potato Trio

Elegant Broccoli and Walnuts

Peppermint Chocolate Cheesecake

Lone Star Barbecue

The Best Barbecued Ribs

Mom's Potato Salad

Onion Bake or Broccoli Slaw

Black Bean Salad

Chocolate Sheet Cake or Cola Cake

Homemade Vanilla Ice Cream

A Taste of Mexico

Chicken Enchilada Casserole or Vegetarian Green Enchiladas

Spicy Salsa

Fabulous Group Salad

Colorado Cornbread

Creole Pralines or Grammy's Wedding Cookies

Praline Cheesecake

The Flavors of Italy

Wonderful Lasagna

Arugula, Tomato and Avocado Salad

Sourdough Bread (not included)

Italian Cream Cake

Meals on Wheels

(For new babies and sick friends)

Option One

Dr. Pepper Meat Loaf

Baked Macaroni and Cheese

Garden Salad with Almonds and Oranges

Martha Howard's Brownies

Option Two

Grilled Pork Tenderloin

Sour Cream Cheese Rice

Spinach-Stuffed Squash

Texas Gold Bars

Option Three

Bow Tie Pasta and
Grilled Chicken Salad

Toasties

Fudge Pie

Option Four

Hot Ham Sandwiches

Fresh Fruit Tray (not included)

Mabel Anne Muhm's Oatmeal
Chocolate Chip Cookies

In the beginning was the Word,
and the Word was made flesh.

John 1:1,14

Jesus once reminded his disciples of an Old Testament scripture when he said, *It is written: 'Man does not live on bread alone, but on every word that comes from the mouth of God'* (Deuteronomy 8:3). Martha Howard is now in her fifty-third year of teaching God's word to her kindergarten Sunday School department. Some of her current students are the children of those she taught years ago. She has shared God's word with hundreds of children, who have been blessed by her teaching and her wonderful Martha Howard Brownies.

Jesus said, *Let the little children come to me, and do not hinder them, for the kingdom of God belongs to such as these* (Matthew 19:14). Many belong to God because of faithful teachers who have shared his word.

Appetizers and Beverages

Heavenly Strawberry Dip

8 ounces cream cheese, softened
$1/2$ cup sour cream
$1/2$ cup sugar
$1/2$ cup packed brown sugar
1 teaspoon cinnamon
1 teaspoon vanilla extract
Fresh strawberries

Combine the cream cheese, sour cream, sugar, brown sugar, cinnamon and vanilla in a bowl. Stir to mix well. Serve with fresh strawberries for dipping.

Yield: $2^1/2$ cups

Roasted Red Pepper Dip

8 ounces cream cheese, softened
1 envelope non-buttermilk ranch salad dressing mix
1 (6-ounce) jar marinated artichoke hearts, drained
$1/3$ cup roasted red peppers, finely chopped
3 tablespoons chopped parsley

Stir the cream cheese and salad dressing mix in a bowl until well blended. Spread $1/3$ of the mixture in the bottom of a bowl lined with plastic wrap. Mix the artichoke hearts, roasted red peppers and parsley in a small bowl. Spread half over the cream cheese layer in the bowl. Spread another $1/3$ of the cream cheese mixture over the vegetables. Top with the remaining vegetables and then spread the remaining cream cheese mixture evenly over the top. Invert the bowl onto a serving plate. Remove the bowl and plastic wrap.

Yield: 12 servings

Crab Dip

8 ounces cream cheese, softened
2 cups sour cream
1 cup mayonnaise
2 tablespoons (or less) seasoned salt
1 tablespoon curry powder
2 teaspoons lemon juice
1 pound crab meat, finely chopped

Combine the cream cheese, sour cream, mayonnaise, seasoned salt, curry powder and lemon juice in a saucepan. Stir to mix well. Heat gently until hot. Fold in the crab meat. Spoon into a bowl and serve warm with crackers.

Yield: 6 cups

Hot Almond Cheese Dip

8 ounces cream cheese, softened
$1/3$ cup mayonnaise
8 ounces Swiss cheese, shredded
4 ounces smoked Gouda cheese, shredded
Dash of pepper
Dash of nutmeg
3 green onions, sliced
$1/3$ to $1/2$ cup sliced almonds

Mix the cream cheese and mayonnaise in a bowl until smooth. Stir in the Swiss cheese, Gouda cheese, pepper and nutmeg. Add the green onions and half the almonds and stir to mix well. Spoon into a baking dish. Bake at 350 degrees for 8 minutes. Sprinkle with the remaining almonds. Bake for 7 to 9 minutes longer.

Yield: 4 cups

Spinach Artichoke Dip

1 (14-ounce) can artichoke hearts, drained well and chopped
1 cup (4 ounces) shredded mozzarella cheese
1 cup (4 ounces) shredded Parmesan cheese
1 cup mayonnaise
1 (10-ounce) package frozen chopped spinach, cooked and drained well
1/4 teaspoon garlic pepper
1/4 teaspoon cayenne pepper
1/4 teaspoon salt

Mix the artichoke hearts, mozzarella cheese, Parmesan cheese, mayonnaise, spinach, garlic pepper, cayenne pepper and salt in a bowl. Spoon into a greased baking dish. Bake at 350 degrees for 20 minutes. Serve with tortilla chips.

Yield: 5 cups

Veggie Dip

6 (4-ounce) cans chopped black olives, drained
6 (4-ounce) cans chopped green chiles, drained
6 tomatoes, chopped
14 green onions, chopped
2 garlic cloves, minced
2 tablespoons olive oil or canola oil
6 tablespoons wine vinegar
4 to 5 tablespoons lemon juice (about 1 large lemon)

Combine the olives, green chiles, tomatoes, green onions and garlic in a large bowl. Whisk the olive oil, vinegar and lemon juice in a small bowl. Pour over the vegetables and toss to mix well. Serve with chips or crackers.

Yield: 12 cups

Hummus

2 (15-ounce) cans garbanzo beans or chick-peas, drained
$^{1}/_{2}$ teaspoon allspice
$^{1}/_{2}$ teaspoon cumin
Dash of garlic powder
$^{1}/_{4}$ cup water
$^{3}/_{4}$ cup tahini (sesame seed paste)
1 cup plain yogurt
4 garlic cloves
Salt to taste
Olive oil

Combine the garbanzo beans, allspice, cumin and garlic powder in a saucepan. Stir in the water. Bring to a boil and reduce the heat. Simmer for 5 minutes. Remove from the heat and let cool. Drain off the liquid. Combine the garbanzo bean mixture, tahini, yogurt and garlic in a food processor. Season with salt. Process until smooth. Spread on a plate and pour a small amount of olive oil on top. Garnish with chopped parsley.

Yield: 4 cups

Let me get you something to eat, so
you can be refreshed and then go on your way.
Genesis 18:5

Spicy Salsa

3 (28-ounce) cans whole tomatoes
1 (14-ounce) can whole tomatoes
1 (12-ounce) jar jalapeño peppers, drained and brine reserved
1 (4-ounce) can chopped green chiles
1 large white onion, chopped
6 garlic cloves
1 bunch fresh cilantro, stems removed
3 tablespoons lemon juice
1 tablespoon cumin
2 teaspoons salt
2 teaspoons coarsely ground pepper

Drain the juice from the cans of tomatoes into a large bowl. Place the tomatoes in a food processor and coarsely chop. Add to the tomato juice. Combine the jalapeño chiles, green chiles, onion, garlic and cilantro in a food processor and coarsely chop. Add to the tomatoes. Stir in the lemon juice, cumin, salt and pepper. Season with the reserved jalapeño chile brine to desired level of heat. Cover and chill.

Yield: 10 cups

They were all encouraged and ate some food themselves.
Acts 27:36

Dott's Cranberry Salsa

1 (12-ounce) bag fresh cranberries, chopped
1 (8-ounce) can crushed pineapple, drained
2/3 cup sugar
1 cup finely chopped green bell pepper
1/2 to 1 bunch fresh cilantro, stems removed and chopped
2 tablespoons finely chopped onion
1 jalapeño chile, seeded and finely chopped
1/4 teaspoon salt

Mix the cranberries, pineapple, sugar, bell pepper, cilantro, onion, jalapeño chile and salt in a bowl. Cover and chill for 2 hours for flavors to blend. Serve with tortilla chips or with your favorite meat.

Yield: 6 cups

Tropical Fruit Salsa

1 ripe papaya, peeled, seeded and chopped
1 ripe mango, peeled, pitted and chopped
1/2 pineapple, peeled, cored and cut into 1/2-inch pieces
2 small red onions, finely chopped
1 jalapeño chile, seeded and finely chopped
1 tablespoon chopped fresh cilantro
1 tablespoon grated lime zest
1 tablespoon fresh lime juice

Mix the papaya, mango, pineapple, onions, jalapeño chile, cilantro, lime zest and lime juice in a bowl. Cover and chill for at least 2 hours.

Yield: 4 cups

Basil Goat Cheese Terrine

8 ounces cream cheese, softened
4 ounces goat cheese
1 cup loosely packed fresh basil leaves
2 garlic cloves, minced
1/4 teaspoon salt
2 tablespoons olive oil
1/4 cup pine nuts, toasted
1 cup (4 ounces) grated Parmesan cheese
1/2 cup sun-dried tomatoes, rehydrated, chopped and
sprinkled with olive oil

Combine the cream cheese and goat cheese in a food processor and process until smooth. Remove to a small bowl. Combine the basil, garlic and salt in a food processor and process until finely chopped. Add the olive oil slowly, processing constantly until smooth. Remove to a bowl and stir in the pine nuts and Parmesan cheese. Spread half the cream cheese mixture in the bottom of a loaf pan lined with plastic wrap. Top with half the sun-dried tomatoes and spread the basil mixture over the sun-dried tomatoes. Top with the remaining sun-dried tomatoes and spread with the remaining cream cheese mixture. Cover with plastic wrap and chill for 24 hours. Invert onto a serving plate. Garnish with basil leaves and serve with crackers.

Yield: 50 servings

Apache Bread

8 ounces cream cheese, softened
$1\frac{1}{2}$ cups (6 ounces) shredded sharp Cheddar cheese
1 cup sour cream
1 (2-ounce) jar dried beef, chopped
1 (4-ounce) can green chiles, drained and chopped
1 round loaf bread, unsliced

Combine the cream cheese, Cheddar cheese, sour cream, dried beef and green chiles in a bowl. Stir to mix well. Cut the top off the bread and hollow out the inside to make room for the dip. Fill the cavity with the cheese mixture and replace the top of the bread. Cover the top with foil and place on a baking sheet. Bake at 350 degrees for $1\frac{1}{2}$ hours. Check after 45 minutes and adjust the temperature if needed. Serve with crackers.

Yield: 32 servings

Cheddar Cheese Ring

16 ounces sharp Cheddar cheese, shredded
1 cup pecans, chopped
$\frac{3}{4}$ cup mayonnaise
1 tablespoon grated onion
$\frac{1}{2}$ teaspoon Tabasco sauce
Strawberry preserves

Combine the cheese, pecans, mayonnaise, onion and Tabasco sauce in a bowl. Stir to mix well. Shape the mixture into a ring on a serving plate. Cover and chill. Fill the center of the ring with strawberry preserves and serve with crackers.

Yield: 24 servings

Blue Cheese Logs

16 ounces cream cheese, softened
1 (8-ounce) package sliced sharp Cheddar cheese, cut into pieces
8 ounces blue cheese, crumbled
1/2 small onion, chopped
4 1/2 teaspoons Worcestershire sauce
1/2 teaspoon cayenne pepper
1 cup finely chopped toasted pecans
1/2 cup finely chopped fresh parsley
1/2 cup finely chopped toasted pecans
1 cup finely chopped fresh parsley

Combine the cream cheese, Cheddar cheese, blue cheese, onion, Worcestershire sauce and cayenne pepper in a food processor. Pulse for 1 to 2 minutes, stopping often to scrape down the sides. Remove to a bowl and stir in 1 cup pecans and 1/2 cup parsley. Cover and chill for 1 hour. Shape into 4 (7-inch-long) logs. Mix 1/2 cup pecans and 1 cup parsley on waxed paper. Roll the logs in the pecan mixture to coat. Cover and chill. Serve with crackers.

Yield: 50 servings

Note: The cheese logs may be frozen. Thaw overnight in the refrigerator before serving.

He makes grass grow for the cattle, and plants
for man to cultivate—bringing forth food from the earth.
Psalm 104:14

Cheese Wafers

8 ounces Cheddar cheese, shredded
3 tablespoons butter, softened
3/4 cup flour
1 teaspoon Worcestershire sauce
1/4 teaspoon salt
1/4 teaspoon Tabasco sauce

Combine the cheese, butter, flour, Worcestershire sauce, salt and Tabasco sauce in a bowl. Stir to mix well. Shape into a 1-inch-diameter log. Wrap tightly in plastic wrap and chill for 30 minutes. Cut into 1/8- to 1/4-inch slices and place on nonstick baking sheets. Bake at 450 degrees for 12 minutes or until golden brown. Remove to a wire rack to cool.

Yield: 4 to 6 dozen wafers

Pecan Cheese in a Pineapple Shell

3/4 cup pecan halves
1 small onion, chopped
2 tablespoons chopped fresh parsley
16 ounces sharp Cheddar cheese, shredded
1 cup mayonnaise
1 whole fresh pineapple
1 jar pineapple preserves

Combine the pecans, onion and parsley in a food processor. Process until finely chopped. Add the cheese and process. Add the mayonnaise and process until well mixed. Lay the pineapple on its side on a cutting board. Cut down the side to remove a lengthwise top. Scoop out the pineapple and reserve for another use. Turn the pineapple over and let drain for at least 1 hour. Spoon the cheese filling into the pineapple shell and top with the pineapple preserves. Serve with butter crackers or an assortment of salty crackers.

Yield: 24 servings

Spinach Feta Cheese Rolls

1 tablespoon olive oil
$^3/_4$ cup thinly sliced green onions
1 (10-ounce) package frozen chopped spinach, thawed and drained well
$1^1/_4$ cups (5 ounces) crumbled feta cheese
1 tablespoon fresh lemon juice
$^1/_4$ teaspoon nutmeg
Salt and pepper to taste
1 egg yolk
1 sheet frozen puff pastry, thawed
Milk

Heat the olive oil in a medium skillet over medium heat. Add the green onions and sauté for 1 minute. Remove to a large bowl and let cool. Stir in the spinach, cheese, lemon juice and nutmeg. Season with salt and pepper. Add the egg yolk and mix well.

Roll out the puff pastry to a 13-inch square on a floured work surface. Cut the pastry in half to make 2 strips. Spread the spinach filling evenly over the 2 strips, leaving a 1-inch border on all sides. Brush the edges of the strips with milk. Roll up each strip, starting with the long side. Press the edges to seal. Place seam side down on a greased baking sheet. Bake at 400 degrees for 25 minutes or until golden brown. Remove to a wire rack to cool.

Yield: 36 servings

Spinach Quesadillas

$1\frac{1}{2}$ teaspoons butter
1 (10-ounce) package frozen chopped spinach, thawed and drained well
4 ounces fresh mushrooms, sliced
Nutmeg to taste
Cayenne pepper to taste
8 ounces cream cheese, softened
8 to 10 large flour tortillas
10 ounces Monterey Jack cheese, shredded

Melt the butter in a large skillet. Add the spinach and mushrooms and sauté lightly. Season with nutmeg and cayenne pepper. Drain if necessary. Stir in the cream cheese. Cook until the cream cheese melts, stirring often. Remove from the heat. Place 4 or 5 tortillas on 1 or 2 baking sheets. Spread the spinach mixture evenly on the tortillas and sprinkle with the Monterey Jack cheese. Top each with a tortilla. Bake at 375 degrees for 7 minutes or until the tortillas are crispy around the edges and the cheese is melted. Cut into quarters and serve hot with sour cream, salsa and guacamole.

Yield: 16 to 20 servings

Brie and Pear Quesadillas

1/4 cup (1/2 stick) butter or margarine
4 large pears, peeled, cored and cut into 1/4-inch slices
1/4 cup sugar
10 large flour tortillas
1/4 cup (1/2 stick) butter, softened
16 ounces Brie cheese, thinly sliced

Melt 1/4 cup butter in a skillet. Add the pears and sauté for 3 minutes. Remove from the heat and sprinkle with the sugar. Let cool. Place 5 tortillas on baking sheets lined with parchment paper. Spread each tortilla with some of the softened butter. Arrange the pears and sliced Brie evenly on top. Cover each with a tortilla. Bake at 350 degrees for 5 minutes. Cut into quarters and serve.

Yield: 20 servings

Note: You may substitute Roquefort cheese for the Brie cheese.

Cucumber Sandwiches

16 ounces cream cheese, softened
2 tablespoons mayonnaise
3 large cucumbers, peeled
1/4 teaspoon dried dill weed or dill seasoning
2 teaspoons lemon juice
Salt to taste
1 long loaf white sandwich bread, or
2 loaves thinly sliced white sandwich bread

Mix the cream cheese and mayonnaise in a bowl until smooth. Grate the cucumbers with a hand grater or in a food processor fitted with the grating blade. Drain well in a colander and then squeeze out all excess moisture with paper towels. Stir into the cream cheese mixture. Add the dill weed and lemon juice and stir to mix well. Season with salt. Spread the filling on a bread slice and top with another bread slice. Repeat with the remaining filling and bread slices. Trim the crusts. Cut sandwiches made from a long bread loaf into 3 fingers. Cut sandwiches made from thinly sliced bread into 2 triangles. Arrange in a single layer in an airtight container. Cover with a slightly damp paper towel. Seal and chill until ready to serve.

Yield: 3 to 4 dozen finger sandwiches

Curried Chicken Tea Sandwiches

$1/2$ cup flaked coconut
$1/2$ cup chopped almonds
8 ounces cream cheese, softened
2 tablespoons orange marmalade
$1\frac{1}{2}$ teaspoons curry powder
$1/4$ teaspoon salt
$1/4$ teaspoon pepper
2 cups chopped cooked chicken
12 slices white bread
3 tablespoons chopped green onions

Spread the coconut and almonds in a shallow baking pan. Bake at 350 degrees for 5 to 10 minutes or until toasted, stirring occasionally. Let cool. Combine the cream cheese, orange marmalade, curry powder, salt and pepper in a bowl. Stir to mix well. Fold in the chicken. Spread evenly on all the bread slices and trim the crusts. Cut each open-face sandwich into 3 strips. Sprinkle with the toasted coconut mixture and green onions.

Yield: 3 dozen finger sandwiches

Crab-Stuffed Mushrooms

1 (6-ounce) can crab meat, drained
2 eggs
2 tablespoons mayonnaise
1/4 cup chopped chives
4 teaspoons lemon juice
1/2 teaspoon Worcestershire sauce
1/4 cup Italian-style seasoned bread crumbs
16 ounces large mushrooms
1/2 cup (1 stick) butter, melted
1/4 cup Italian-style seasoned bread crumbs

Mix the crab meat, eggs, mayonnaise, chives, lemon juice, Worcestershire sauce and 1/4 cup bread crumbs in a bowl. Remove the stems from the mushrooms and reserve for another use. Dip the mushroom caps in the melted butter and place top down in a baking dish coated with nonstick cooking spray. Fill the caps with the crab mixture. Sprinkle with 1/4 cup bread crumbs. Pour the remaining melted butter evenly over the stuffed mushrooms. Bake at 350 degrees for 15 to 20 minutes.

Yield: 6 to 8 servings

Almond Tea

3 regular tea bags, or 1 family-size tea bag
2 cups boiling water
$^1/_2$ cup plus 2 tablespoons lemon juice
1 tablespoon vanilla extract
1 tablespoon almond extract
1 cup sugar
4 cups water

Combine the tea bags and the boiling water in a saucepan and let steep. Remove the tea bags. Stir in the lemon juice, vanilla, almond extract and sugar. Cook for 5 minutes. Stir in 4 cups water. Serve hot or chilled.

Yield: 7 to 8 cups

Delta Mint Tea

7 tea bags
12 fresh mint sprigs
Zest of 3 lemons
8 cups boiling water
Juice of 7 lemons
2 cups sugar
8 cups water

Combine the tea bags, mint, lemon zest and boiling water in a large bowl. Let steep for 12 minutes. Strain the liquid into a large bowl or pitcher. Add the lemon juice and sugar and stir until the sugar dissolves. Stir in 8 cups water.

Yield: 1 gallon

Gilmer Tea

5 tablespoons unsweetened instant tea
8 cups water
1 (46-ounce) can pineapple juice
1 (12-ounce) can frozen orange juice concentrate, reconstituted
1 (6-ounce) can frozen lemonade concentrate, reconstituted
3 cups sugar
2 cups water
2 tablespoons whole cloves
4 cinnamon sticks

Dissolve the instant tea in 8 cups water in a very large saucepan. Stir in the pineapple juice, orange juice, lemonade and sugar. Combine 2 cups water, the cloves and cinnamon sticks in a small saucepan. Bring to a boil. Remove from the heat and cover. Let steep for a few minutes. Strain the liquid into the tea mixture. Heat until hot but do not boil, stirring occasionally.

Yield: $1^1/_2$ gallons

Share with God's people that are in need. Practice hospitality.
Romans 12:13

Pineapple Tea

1/4 cup unsweetened instant tea
2 cups sugar
4 cups boiling water
8 cups unsweetened pineapple juice
3 cups water
1 cup lemon juice
14 maraschino cherries
14 pineapple chunks

Combine the instant tea and sugar in a very large heatproof bowl or pitcher. Add the boiling water and stir until the sugar dissolves. Stir in the pineapple juice, 3 cups water and lemon juice. Cover and chill.

Pour 1/4 inch water into the bottom of each section of 2 ice cube trays. Freeze until firm. Place 1 maraschino cherry in the center of each cube in 1 tray. Place 1 pineapple chunk in the center of each cube in the other tray. Pour 1/4 inch water into each section over the fruit and freeze until firm. Add additional water to the sections to fill. Freeze until firm. Place the fruit ice cubes in glasses and add the chilled tea. Garnish with fresh mint.

Yield: 17 cups

Hot Spiced Cider

1 (12-ounce) can frozen cranberry juice cocktail concentrate, reconstituted
1 (12-ounce) can frozen apple juice concentrate, reconstituted
1/2 cup packed brown sugar
2 or 3 cinnamon sticks
1 teaspoon whole cloves

Pour the cranberry juice cocktail and apple juice into the base of a 30-cup coffee percolator. Place the brown sugar, cinnamon sticks and cloves in the clean basket and set in the percolator. Run through a standard cycle and serve hot.

Yield: 12 cups

Variation: For a non-red cider, substitute pineapple juice for the cranberry juice cocktail and increase the brown sugar to 1 cup.

Orange Wassail

8 cups orange juice
8 cups apple juice
4 cups cranberry juice cocktail
1 (12-ounce) can frozen lemonade concentrate, thawed
1 (2-inch) cinnamon stick
1 tablespoon whole cloves
2 oranges, sliced

Combine the orange juice, apple juice, cranberry juice cocktail, lemonade concentrate and cinnamon stick in a large saucepan. Insert the cloves into the orange slices and add to the juices. Cook over medium-high heat until heated through. Serve hot.

Yield: 21 cups

I am the way, the truth, and the life:
no man cometh unto the Father, but by me.

John 14:6

Kathleen York was the first bride at Park Cities Baptist Church and a faithful servant of the Lord. Kathleen established the International Friends ministry, which still teaches adults English as a second language. She also taught two-year-olds in Sunday School for more than fifty years. Her close friend, Virginia Presley, began the Clothes Closet Ministry at Park Cities, and together these two dedicated women volunteered for many years at Brother Bill's Helping Hand in West Dallas. They shared their time with others, even as they shared many gallons of Tutti-Frutti Ice Cream and Gilmer Tea.

Their lives were a testimony of Christ as the way, the truth, and the life, and many came to the Father because they saw Jesus in these women.

Breakfasts and Breads

Crescent Sausage Roll

2 (8-ounce) cans refrigerator crescent rolls
8 ounces cream cheese, softened
2 pounds hot bulk sausage, browned, drained and crumbled

Unroll the crescent roll dough on a floured work surface. Press the seams together on each to form 2 rectangles. Stir the cream cheese and cooked sausage in a bowl until well mixed. Spread evenly on the dough. Roll up each to form a log. Place seam side down on a nonstick baking sheet. Bake at 350 degrees for 15 to 20 minutes or until golden brown. Remove to a wire rack to cool.

Yield: 12 servings

Pull-Apart Breakfast Bread

1 cup (2 sticks) margarine
3/4 cup chopped onion
3/4 cup chopped green bell pepper
3 (7-ounce) cans refrigerator biscuits
8 ounces bacon or sausage, cooked, drained and crumbled
1/2 to 1 cup (2 to 4 ounces) grated Parmesan cheese

Melt the margarine in a saucepan. Add the onion and bell pepper and sauté until tender. Remove the vegetables and liquid to a large bowl. Separate the biscuit dough and cut each biscuit into quarters. Add to the vegetables. Stir in the cooked bacon and cheese and mix well. Spoon into a nonstick bundt pan. Bake at 350 degrees for 30 minutes. Cool in the pan for 10 minutes. Invert onto a serving plate.

Yield: 12 servings

Note: This may be prepared ahead. Cover and chill overnight before baking.

Sausage Spinach Quiche

8 ounces sausage
3 tablespoons chopped onion
3 tablespoons sliced mushrooms
1 (12-ounce) frozen spinach soufflé, thawed
2 eggs, beaten
3 tablespoons milk
1 cup (4 ounces) shredded Swiss cheese
1 unbaked (9-inch) pie shell

Sauté the sausage, onion and mushrooms in a skillet until the sausage is brown. Drain and place in a bowl. Add the spinach soufflé, eggs, milk and cheese. Stir to mix well. Pour into the pie shell. Bake at 450 degrees for 35 to 40 minutes. Remove to a wire rack to cool.

Yield: 6 to 8 servings

Sausage Egg Casserole

9 eggs
3 cups milk
1 1/2 teaspoons dry mustard
1/2 teaspoon salt
2 pounds sausage, browned, drained and crumbled
3 slices white bread, torn into pieces
1 1/2 cups (6 ounces) shredded Monterey Jack cheese

Beat the eggs, milk, dry mustard and salt in a bowl. Add the cooked sausage, bread pieces and cheese and stir to mix well. Spoon into a 3-quart baking dish. Cover and chill overnight. Bake at 350 degrees for 1 hour.

Yield: 12 servings

Easter Brunch Spinach and Eggs

8 ounces cream cheese
1 (10-ounce) can cream of mushroom soup
12 ounces Monterey Jack cheese, shredded
$^1/_4$ cup ($^1/_2$ stick) butter, cut into pieces
3 (10-ounce) packages frozen creamed spinach, thawed
Milk (optional)
Bread crumbs
7 or 8 hard-cooked eggs, sliced

Place the cream cheese in a large microwave-safe bowl. Microwave until the cheese is melted. Stir in the soup gradually. Add the Monterey Jack cheese and butter and stir to mix. Add the creamed spinach and mix well. Microwave until the mixture is hot and the cheese is melted, stirring every 2 minutes. Thin with milk if necessary. Coat a 9×13-inch baking dish with nonstick cooking spray. Coat with bread crumbs. Arrange the egg slices in the bottom of the baking dish. Pour the cheese mixture over the eggs. Top with bread crumbs. Bake at 350 degrees until hot and bubbly.

Yield: 12 servings

Caramel French Toast

1½ cups packed brown sugar
¾ cup (1½ sticks) butter
6 tablespoons corn syrup
10 (1-inch-thick) slices French bread
4 eggs, beaten
2½ cups milk
1 tablespoon vanilla extract
¼ teaspoon salt
3 tablespoons sugar
1½ teaspoons cinnamon
¼ cup (½ stick) butter, melted

Combine the brown sugar, ¾ cup butter and corn syrup in a saucepan. Cook over medium heat for 5 minutes or until the mixture is bubbly, stirring constantly. Pour the syrup evenly over the bottom of a lightly greased 9×13-inch baking dish. Arrange the bread slices on top of the syrup. Beat the eggs, milk, vanilla and salt in a bowl. Pour slowly over the bread. Cover and chill for at least 8 hours. Mix the sugar and cinnamon in a small bowl. Sprinkle over the bread. Drizzle with the melted butter. Bake at 350 degrees for 45 to 50 minutes or until golden brown and bubbly. Serve immediately.

Yield: 12 servings

Cinnamon Rolls

1 cup milk
1 cup water
1/2 cup shortening
2 envelopes dry yeast
1/2 cup sugar
1 tablespoon salt
4 1/2 cups flour
1/2 cup (1 stick) butter, melted
Cinnamon
Sugar
1/4 cup milk
1/4 teaspoon vanilla extract
Confectioners' sugar

Combine 1 cup milk, the water and shortening in a saucepan. Heat until the shortening melts and the mixture is warm but not hot. Combine the yeast, 1/2 cup sugar and salt in a large bowl. Add the warm liquid and beat slowly for 2 minutes. Stir in the flour gradually until a stiff dough forms. Turn the dough out onto a floured work surface and divide into 2 balls. Roll out each ball to a 9×12-inch rectangle. Brush each with the melted butter. Mix cinnamon and sugar in a small bowl. Sprinkle generously over the dough. Roll up each strip, starting with the long side. Press the edges to seal. Cut into slices and place in a greased baking pan. Cover and let rise for 1 hour or until doubled in bulk. Bake at 350 degrees for 30 minutes or until light brown. Remove to a wire rack to cool slightly. Mix 1/4 cup milk, the vanilla and enough confectioners' sugar to make a thin icing in a bowl. Drizzle over the warm rolls.

Yield: 24 rolls

Overnight Cinnamon Rolls

3/4 cup chopped pecans (optional)
18 frozen dinner rolls
1/2 cup (1 stick) butter, melted
1/2 cup packed brown sugar
1 (4-ounce) package vanilla pudding mix (not instant)
1 teaspoon cinnamon

Coat a greased bundt pan with the pecans. Arrange the rolls evenly in the pan. Mix the remaining ingredients in a bowl. Pour over the frozen rolls. Cover loosely and let stand at room temperature overnight. Bake at 350 degrees for 25 minutes. Cool in the pan for 10 minutes. Invert onto a serving plate and serve by pulling apart.

Yield: 12 servings

Sticky Buns

1 cup packed brown sugar
1/2 to 3/4 cup chopped pecans
1 cup maple syrup or dark corn syrup
1/4 cup (1/2 stick) butter or margarine, melted
8 ounces cream cheese, softened
1/4 cup confectioners' sugar
2 tablespoons butter or margarine, softened
2 (10-ounce) cans refrigerator flaky biscuits

Mix the brown sugar, pecans, maple syrup and melted butter in a bowl. Spread in the bottom of an ungreased 8×12-inch or 9×13-inch baking pan. Mix the cream cheese, confectioners' sugar and softened butter in a bowl until smooth. Separate the biscuits on a work surface. Flatten each into a 4-inch circle. Spoon 1 tablespoon of the cream cheese filling in the center of each circle. Overlap the dough to form finger-shaped rolls. Place seam side down in rows of 10 in the baking dish. Bake at 350 degrees for 20 to 30 minutes or until deep golden brown. Invert onto a serving plate and serve warm.

Yield: 20 buns

New Orleans Creole Biscuits

3 cups flour, sifted
1 tablespoon baking powder
1 tablespoon sugar
1 teaspoon salt
1/4 cup (1/2 stick) margarine, softened
1 1/2 cups buttermilk

Mix the flour, baking powder, sugar and salt in a bowl. Cut in the margarine with a pastry blender or fork. Stir in the buttermilk. Knead the dough on a floured work surface and pat to 1/2 inch thick. Cut with a biscuit cutter. Place on an ungreased baking sheet. Bake at 350 degrees for 25 to 30 minutes or until golden brown. Remove to a wire rack to cool.

Yield: 12 biscuits

Poppy Seed Muffins

3 cups flour
2 cups sugar
3 eggs
1 1/2 teaspoons baking powder
1 teaspoon salt
4 1/2 teaspoons poppy seeds
1 1/2 cups milk
3/4 cup vegetable oil or canola oil
1 1/2 teaspoons vanilla extract
1 1/2 teaspoons almond extract

Combine the flour, sugar, eggs, baking powder, salt, poppy seeds, milk, oil, vanilla and almond extract in a mixing bowl. Beat with an electric mixer at medium speed for 2 minutes. Spoon into well-greased muffin cups. Bake at 400 degrees for 20 to 25 minutes or until a wooden pick inserted in the center comes out clean. Cool in the pan for 5 minutes. Remove to a wire rack to cool completely.

Yield: 24 muffins

Zucchini Nut Muffins

2 eggs, lightly beaten
1/2 cup packed brown sugar
1/2 cup honey
1/2 cup (1 stick) butter or margarine, melted
1 teaspoon vanilla extract
1 3/4 cups flour
1 teaspoon baking soda
1 teaspoon salt (optional)
1/2 teaspoon baking powder
1 1/2 teaspoons cinnamon
1/2 teaspoon nutmeg
1 cup granola
1/2 cup nuts, chopped
2 cups shredded zucchini

Beat the eggs, brown sugar, honey, melted butter and vanilla in a large bowl. Mix the flour, baking soda, salt, baking powder, cinnamon and nutmeg in a bowl. Add the dry ingredients to the egg mixture and stir just until moistened. Fold in the granola, nuts and zucchini. Fill greased muffin cups 3/4 full. Bake at 350 degrees for 20 to 25 minutes or until a wooden pick inserted in the center comes out clean. Cool in the pan for 5 minutes. Remove to a wire rack. Serve warm; or cool completely, wrap airtight and freeze.

Yield: 18 muffins

Blueberry Coffee Cake

1 cup (2 sticks) butter, softened
2 cups sugar
2 eggs
1 cup sour cream
1/2 teaspoon vanilla extract
1 1/2 cups plus 2 tablespoons flour
1 teaspoon baking powder
1/4 teaspoon salt
1 cup fresh blueberries or thawed frozen blueberries
1/2 cup packed brown sugar
1 teaspoon cinnamon
1/2 cup chopped pecans
Confectioners' sugar

Cream the butter and sugar in a mixing bowl until light and fluffy. Beat in the eggs. Add the sour cream and vanilla and beat well. Mix the flour, baking powder and salt in a bowl. Beat into the butter mixture. Fold in the blueberries. Pour half the batter into a greased and floured bundt pan. Mix the brown sugar, cinnamon and pecans in a bowl. Sprinkle over the batter in the pan. Top with the remaining batter. Bake at 350 degrees for 50 to 60 minutes or until a wooden pick inserted in the center comes out clean. Remove to a wire rack and let cool in the pan. Invert onto a serving plate and sift confectioners' sugar over the top.

Yield: 12 servings

The Closet Coffee Cake

1 (18-ounce) box deluxe yellow cake mix
1 (3-ounce) package vanilla instant pudding mix
1 cup vegetable oil
4 eggs
1 teaspoon vanilla extract
1 cup sour cream
1/2 cup sugar
1/2 cup packed brown sugar
1/2 cup (1 stick) margarine, melted
6 tablespoons flour
2 teaspoons cinnamon

Combine the cake mix, pudding mix, oil, eggs, vanilla and sour cream in a bowl. Beat with an electric mixer at medium speed for 2 minutes. Pour half the batter into a greased and floured 9×13-inch baking pan. Mix the sugar, brown sugar, melted margarine, flour and cinnamon in a bowl. Sprinkle half over the batter in the pan. Top with the remaining batter and sprinkle with the remaining sugar mixture. Bake at 350 degrees for 45 minutes or until a wooden pick inserted in the center comes out clean. Remove to a wire rack to cool.

Yield: 15 servings

Banana Bread

$^1/_2$ cup (1 stick) butter, softened
1 cup sugar
2 eggs, well beaten
2 cups mashed bananas (about 4 medium bananas)
2 cups flour
1 teaspoon baking soda
Pinch of salt
1 cup chopped pecans (optional)

Combine the butter, sugar, eggs, bananas, flour, baking soda, salt and pecans in a bowl. Stir to mix well. Pour into a greased loaf or bundt pan. Bake at 350 degrees for 1 hour or until a wooden pick inserted in the center comes out clean. Cool in the pan for 5 minutes. Remove to a wire rack to cool completely.

Yield: 12 servings

Cranberry Bread

1 cup (2 sticks) butter, softened
2 cups sugar
4 eggs
2 cups flour
1 teaspoon vanilla extract
$^1/_2$ cup evaporated milk
1 cup chopped pecans
1 cup chopped fresh cranberries

Cream the butter and sugar in a bowl with an electric mixer. Add the eggs 1 at a time, beating well after each addition. Beat in the flour, vanilla and evaporated milk. Fold in the pecans and cranberries. Pour into a greased loaf or tube pan. Bake at 325 degrees for 1 hour or until a wooden pick inserted in the center comes out clean. Cool in the pan for 5 minutes. Remove to a wire rack and let cool completely.

Yield: 12 servings

Strawberry Nut Bread

3 cups flour
1 teaspoon baking soda
1 teaspoon salt
1 tablespoon cinnamon
2 cups sugar
4 eggs, beaten
$1^1/_4$ cups vegetable oil
2 cups frozen strawberries with juice, thawed
$1^1/_4$ cups pecans, chopped

Combine the flour, baking soda, salt, cinnamon, sugar, eggs, oil, strawberries and pecans in a large bowl. Stir just until moistened. Spoon into 2 well-greased loaf pans. Bake at 350 degrees for 60 to 70 minutes or until a wooden pick inserted in the center comes out clean. Cool in the pans for 10 minutes. Remove to a wire rack to cool completely.

Yield: 12 servings

Toasties

1 (12-ounce) package French rolls
1 cup (2 sticks) butter, melted
Garlic powder
Dried basil
Dried parsley flakes
Paprika
Grated Parmesan cheese

Slice the rolls into halves lengthwise and brush with melted butter. Sprinkle with garlic powder, basil, parsley, paprika and Parmesan cheese. Place on a baking sheet. Bake at 250 degrees for 45 minutes. Serve warm.

Yield: 12 servings

Colorado Corn Bread

1 cup (2 sticks) butter, softened
1 cup sugar
4 eggs
2 cups cream-style corn
1/2 cup (2 ounces) shredded Monterey Jack cheese
1/2 cup (2 ounces) shredded Cheddar cheese
1 cup flour
1 cup yellow cornmeal
4 teaspoons baking powder
1/4 teaspoon salt

Cream the butter and sugar in a bowl with an electric mixer. Add the eggs 1 at a time, beating well after each addition. Stir in the corn, Monterey Jack cheese and Cheddar cheese. Mix the flour, cornmeal, baking powder and salt in a bowl. Add to the cheese mixture and stir to mix well. Spread evenly in a greased 9×13-inch baking pan. Place in a 350-degree oven. Reduce the temperature to 300 degrees and bake for 1 hour or until the center is set and the top looks moist. Remove to a wire rack. Serve warm.

Yield: 15 servings

If your enemy is hungry, give him food
to eat; if he is thirsty, give him water to drink.
Proverbs 25:21

Herbed Rolls

1/2 cup (1 stick) butter or margarine
1 1/2 teaspoons dried parsley flakes
1/2 teaspoon dried dill weed
1 teaspoon dried onion flakes
2 teaspoons grated Parmesan cheese
1 (10-count) can refrigerator buttermilk biscuits

Melt the butter in a 9- or 10-inch round baking pan. Add the parsley, dill weed, onion flakes and cheese and stir to mix. Let stand for 30 minutes. Cut each biscuit in half. Place in the pan and turn to coat all sides with the herb mixture. Bake at 425 degrees for 12 to 15 minutes.

Yield: 10 servings

Dinner Rolls

3 eggs, beaten
1 teaspoon (heaping) salt
1/2 cup sugar
1/2 cup (1 stick) butter, melted
1 cup warm water
1 envelope cake yeast
4 1/2 cups flour
Melted butter

Combine the eggs, salt, sugar, melted butter, warm water and yeast in a large bowl. Stir until the yeast dissolves. Stir in the flour to form a dough. Let rise for 4 hours. Cover and chill overnight. Roll out half the dough on a floured work surface. Cut into circles and dip into melted butter. Fold each in half and arrange in a pie plate. Let rise for 4 hours or until doubled in bulk. Bake at 350 degrees for 15 minutes or until golden brown.

Yield: 3 dozen rolls

For by grace are ye saved through faith;
it is the gift of God.

Ephesians 2:8

The church has grown considerably since its early beginnings, but it has maintained a commitment to be a true family of faith that shares the gift of God's grace with all. Youth have always been important members of that family. In the early years, there were Crusader Choir parties for the high school students at the home of Lou Yarborough, and a Sunday School party at Mabel Anne Muhm's meant Oatmeal Chocolate Chip Cookies just waiting to be devoured.

God's grace is a gift to be received through faith and then given to others. Many have been blessed by those who were so willing to share the grace they had received.

Soups and Salads

Austin Cheese Soup

2 cups (4 sticks) margarine
$1\frac{1}{2}$ cups finely chopped onions
2 cups finely chopped carrots
2 cups finely chopped celery
1 cup flour
$\frac{1}{2}$ teaspoon baking soda
$\frac{1}{4}$ cup cornstarch
16 cups milk, warmed
4 (10-ounce) cans chicken broth
4 pounds Cheddar cheese, shredded
1 tablespoon salt
1 tablespoon black pepper
2 teaspoons dried parsley flakes
1 to 2 dashes of cayenne pepper and/or paprika

Melt the margarine in a very large saucepan. Add the onions, carrots and celery and sauté until tender. Stir in the flour, baking soda and cornstarch. Cook until bubbly, stirring constantly. Stir in the milk and chicken broth gradually. Cook until thickened, stirring constantly. Add the cheese and cook until melted, stirring often. Add the salt, black pepper, parsley, cayenne pepper and paprika and stir to mix.

Yield: 25 servings

Cheesy Vegetable Chowder

1/2 cup chopped onion
1 garlic clove, minced
1 cup sliced celery
3/4 cup sliced carrots
1 cup cubed potatoes
3 1/2 cups chicken broth
1 (17-ounce) can whole kernel corn
1/4 cup (1/2 stick) margarine
1/4 cup flour
2 cups milk
1 tablespoon prepared mustard
1/2 teaspoon paprika
1/4 teaspoon pepper
2 tablespoons chopped pimentos
2 cups (8 ounces) shredded Cheddar cheese

Combine the onion, garlic, celery, carrots, potatoes and chicken broth in a large saucepan. Bring to a boil. Cover and reduce the heat. Simmer for 20 minutes. Stir in the corn and remove from the heat. Melt the margarine in a heavy saucepan over low heat. Add the flour and stir until smooth. Cook for 1 minute. Stir in the milk gradually. Cook until thick, stirring constantly. Add the mustard, paprika, pepper, pimentos and cheese. Cook until the cheese melts, stirring often. Add to the vegetable mixture. Cook until hot, stirring often.

Yield: 8 servings

Poblano Corn Chowder

½ cup (1 stick) butter
5 poblano chiles, seeded and chopped
2 small onions, chopped
3 garlic cloves, minced
2 (14-ounce) cans chicken broth
4 (14-ounce) cans cream-style corn
3 tablespoons chicken bouillon granules
3 tablespoons cumin
2 to 3 teaspoons pepper
3 tablespoons chopped fresh parsley
3 tablespoons chopped fresh cilantro
4 cups half-and-half
Shredded Monterey Jack cheese

Melt the butter in a large saucepan. Add the poblano chiles, onions and garlic and sauté until tender. Stir in the chicken broth, corn, bouillon granules, cumin, pepper, parsley and cilantro. Simmer for 1 hour. Stir in the half-and-half. Cook just until heated through. Ladle into bowls and top with shredded Monterey Jack cheese.

Yield: 12 servings

Baked Potato Soup

6 to 8 large potatoes
2 cups chicken stock
1/2 cup (1 stick) butter
1/2 yellow onion, chopped
1/4 cup flour
1 tablespoon chopped fresh parsley
3/4 teaspoon white pepper (or to taste)
1 teaspoon garlic paste
1 teaspoon salt (or to taste)
10 drops of jalapeño pepper sauce
2 cups milk or cream

Scrub the potatoes and prick with a fork. Bake at 375 degrees for 1 hour or until done. Cut into halves. Remove the cooked potatoes and discard the skins. Cut the cooked potatoes into 1/4- to 1/2-inch pieces. Place 2 cups of the potato pieces in a food processor. Add the chicken stock and process until smooth and creamy. Melt the butter in a large saucepan over medium heat. Add the onion and sauté until tender. Stir in the flour. Cook until bubbly, stirring constantly. Add the puréed potato mixture, remaining potato pieces, parsley, white pepper, garlic paste, salt, pepper sauce and milk. Simmer for 30 to 45 minutes. Add more seasoning, if desired. Ladle into bowls and garnish with shredded Cheddar cheese, crumbled bacon and chopped green onions.

Yield: 6 servings

Minestrone

4 garlic cloves, minced
1 onion, finely chopped
2 ribs celery, chopped
6 cups chicken broth
1 (14-ounce) can diced tomatoes
1 tablespoon olive oil
3 fresh basil sprigs, chopped, or 1 tablespoon dried basil
1 tablespoon dried oregano
2 teaspoons salt
1/2 teaspoon pepper
3 unpeeled red-skinned potatoes, cubed
2 carrots, chopped
1 (10-ounce) package frozen green beans, cooked tender-crisp
1 (15-ounce) can cannellini beans, rinsed and drained
2 cups cooked elbow macaroni

Combine the garlic, onion, celery, chicken broth, tomatoes, olive oil, basil, oregano, salt and pepper in a large saucepan. Bring to a boil. Add the potatoes and carrots. Reduce the heat and simmer for 30 to 45 minutes. Stir in the green beans, cannellini beans and macaroni. Cook until heated through.

Yield: 8 servings

Tortilla Soup

2 tablespoons vegetable oil
1 onion, chopped
1/4 to 1/2 jalapeño chile, seeded and chopped
2 garlic cloves, minced
1 (14-ounce) can whole tomatoes
1 (5-ounce) can diced tomatoes with green chiles
2 (10-ounce) cans beef broth
2 (10-ounce) cans chicken broth
1 (10-ounce) can tomato soup
2 cups water or chicken broth
1 teaspoon cumin
1 teaspoon chili powder
1 teaspoon salt (optional)
2 teaspoons Worcestershire sauce
1/2 teaspoon lemon pepper
4 chicken breasts, cooked and cut into 1/4-inch strips
4 teaspoons chopped fresh cilantro
1 avocado, peeled, pitted and sliced
1 cup sour cream
1 (12-ounce) package corn tortillas, cut into strips and fried crisp in oil
10 ounces Monterey Jack cheese, shredded

Heat the oil in a large saucepan. Add the onion, jalapeño chile and garlic. Sauté until tender. Stir in the whole tomatoes, tomatoes with green chiles, beef broth, chicken broth, tomato soup, water, cumin, chili powder, salt, Worcestershire sauce and lemon pepper. Simmer for 50 minutes. Add the cooked chicken and simmer for 10 to 15 minutes. Stir in the cilantro. Ladle into serving bowls. Top each with some of the avocado, sour cream, fried tortilla strips and cheese.

Yield: 12 servings

Chili

1 pound lean ground beef
1 large onion, chopped
2 tablespoons chili powder
1 teaspoon baking cocoa
Garlic to taste
Salt to taste
1 (15-ounce) can red kidney beans
1 (16-ounce) can ranch-style beans
1 (16-ounce) can pinto beans
1 (14-ounce) can tomatoes
Butter or margarine (optional)

Brown the ground beef with the onion in a large saucepan, stirring until the ground beef is crumbly; drain. Stir in the chili powder and baking cocoa. Season with garlic and salt. Simmer for a few minutes. Stir in the kidney beans, ranch-style beans, pinto beans and tomatoes. Simmer until the desired thickness is reached. Ladle into serving bowls and top each with a small amount of butter.

Yield: 6 servings

Sonoran Chicken Chili

1 tablespoon olive oil
1/2 cup chopped shallots
3 garlic cloves, minced
2 (14-ounce) cans chopped tomatoes with garlic, oregano and basil
1 (14-ounce) can whole tomatoes, chopped
1 (14-ounce) can no-salt-added chicken broth
1 (4-ounce) can chopped green chiles
1/2 teaspoon oregano
1/2 teaspoon coriander
1/4 teaspoon cumin
4 cups chopped cooked chicken
1 to 2 (16-ounce) cans white kidney or navy beans, drained
3 tablespoons fresh lime juice
1/4 teaspoon freshly ground pepper

Heat the olive oil in a large saucepan over medium-high heat. Add the shallots and garlic. Sauté for 5 minutes or until tender. Stir in the seasoned tomatoes, chopped tomatoes, chicken broth, green chiles, oregano, coriander and cumin. Bring to a boil. Reduce the heat and simmer for 20 minutes. Stir in the chicken and kidney beans. Cook just until heated through. Stir in the lime juice and pepper. Ladle into serving bowls and garnish with shredded Cheddar cheese.

Yield: 8 servings

Santa Fe Stew

2 pounds ground beef or turkey
2 large onions, chopped
2 (15-ounce) cans kidney beans
2 (16-ounce) cans pinto beans
2 (15-ounce) cans whole kernel corn
2 (14-ounce) cans seasoned tomatoes
1 (10-ounce) can tomatoes with green chiles
2 envelopes taco seasoning mix
1 envelope ranch salad dressing mix

Brown the ground beef in a large saucepan, stirring until crumbly; drain. Add the onions and cook until tender. Stir in the kidney beans, pinto beans, corn, seasoned tomatoes and tomatoes with green chiles. Bring to a boil. Reduce the heat and add the taco seasoning mix and salad dressing mix. Stir to mix well. Cover and simmer for at least 30 minutes.

Yield: 8 servings

Offer hospitality to one another without grumbling.
I Peter 4:9

Bok Choy Salad

Salad

1 large head napa cabbage, torn into bite-size pieces
1 bunch bok choy, bottom part only, chopped
1/2 head red cabbage, shredded
1 red bell pepper, seeded and cut into thin strips
2 carrots, thinly sliced lengthwise
1 small bunch green onions, chopped
3 to 4 tablespoons chopped fresh cilantro
1 tablespoon finely chopped fresh mint
1 tablespoon butter
1 (3-ounce) package ramen noodles (discard the seasoning packet)
1 package spicy Szechuan almonds (found in the produce section)
1 (2-ounce) jar toasted sesame seeds (found in the Asian food section)

Dressing

3 tablespoons soy sauce
1/4 cup rice vinegar
1/4 cup sweet chile sauce
1/2 cup sugar
3/4 cup sesame oil
Lime juice to taste (optional)

For the salad, combine the napa cabbage, bok choy, red cabbage, bell pepper, carrots, green onions, cilantro and mint in a large bowl. Melt the butter in a skillet. Add the ramen noodles and sauté until light brown. Remove from the heat and stir in the almonds and sesame seeds. Add to the salad and toss to mix.

For the dressing, combine the soy sauce, vinegar, chile sauce, sugar and sesame oil in a jar with a tight-fitting lid. Season with lime juice. Shake until well mixed. Add the desired amount to the salad and toss to coat.

Yield: 4 to 6 servings

Note: Strips of grilled chicken breast may be added to the salad. You may substitute 1/2 cup ground toasted cocktail peanuts for the sesame seeds.

Arugula, Tomato and Avocado Salad

8 cups loosely packed arugula, torn into bite-size pieces
16 ounces plum tomatoes, chopped
4 stalks canned hearts of palm, sliced
2 avocados, peeled, pitted and chopped
5 tablespoons extra-virgin olive oil
3 tablespoons fresh lemon juice
Salt and pepper to taste
1 (12-ounce) wedge Parmesan cheese
1/4 cup pine nuts, toasted

Combine the arugula, tomatoes, hearts of palm and avocados in a large bowl. Whisk the olive oil and lemon juice in a small bowl. Season with salt and pepper. Add to the salad and toss to coat. Shave strips of the Parmesan cheese over the salad using a vegetable peeler. Sprinkle with the pine nuts.

Yield: 4 servings

So Abraham said to Sarah, "Quick, get three seahs of fine flour and knead it and bake some bread."
Genesis 18:6

Field Greens and Crumbled Blue Cheese Salad

4 cups mixed field greens
2 green onions, chopped
4 ounces blue cheese, crumbled (about 1 cup)
1 Granny Smith apple, cored and chopped
Vinaigrette (below)

Combine the field greens, green onions, blue cheese and apple in a large bowl. Toss to mix. Add the Vinaigrette and toss to coat.

Yield: 8 servings

Vinaigrette

2/3 cup sugar
1 teaspoon dry mustard
1 teaspoon salt
2/3 cup white vinegar
3 tablespoons cider vinegar
4 1/2 teaspoons onion juice
2 tablespoons Worcestershire sauce
1 cup vegetable oil

Mix the sugar, dry mustard, salt, white vinegar and cider vinegar in a bowl. Stir until the sugar dissolves. Whisk in the onion juice and Worcestershire sauce. Whisk in the oil gradually until blended.

Yield: 2 1/2 cups

Italian Tossed Salad

Salt
1 garlic clove, cut
1/4 cup olive oil
1 tablespoon each lemon juice or wine vinegar and mayonnaise
1 teaspoon dry mustard
Freshly ground pepper
1 head romaine, torn into bite-size pieces
1 bulb fennel, julienned (optional)
1/3 cup walnuts, coarsely chopped
1 tablespoon capers
2 hard-cooked eggs, sliced
Grated Parmesan cheese (optional)

Sprinkle the bottom of a salad bowl with salt and rub with the cut garlic clove. Discard the garlic. Add the next 5 ingredients to the bowl. Stir with a wooden spoon until well blended. Add the romaine, fennel, walnuts, capers and eggs. Toss gently with a fork and spoon. Sprinkle with Parmesan cheese.

Yield: 6 servings

Bibb Salad with Raspberry Maple Dressing

5 heads Bibb lettuce, torn into pieces
2 small purple onions, sliced and separated into rings
2 cups (8ounces) crumbled blue cheese or feta cheese
1/2 cup toasted pine nuts or sunflower seeds
2/3 cup vegetable oil
1/4 cup raspberry vinegar
2 tablespoons maple syrup

Arrange the lettuce and onion rings on 12 salad plates. Sprinkle evenly with the blue cheese and pine nuts. Combine the oil, vinegar and maple syrup in a jar with a tight-fitting lid. Shake until well mixed. Drizzle the desired amount over the salads.

Yield: 12 servings

Garden Salad with Almonds and Oranges

Dressing

1 cup vegetable oil
1/4 cup balsamic vinegar
1/4 cup sugar
1 tablespoon dried parsley flakes
1 teaspoon salt
Dash of black pepper
Dash of cayenne pepper

Salad

1 cup sliced or slivered almonds
1/4 cup sugar
1 head romaine, torn into bite-size pieces
1 head leafy green or iceberg lettuce, torn into bite-size pieces
6 green onion tops, thinly sliced
2 (11-ounce) cans mandarin oranges, chilled and well drained

For the dressing, whisk the oil, vinegar, sugar, parsley, salt, black pepper and cayenne pepper in a bowl until blended. Cover and chill.

For the salad, combine the almonds and sugar in a saucepan. Cook over medium heat until the sugar melts and is golden brown, stirring constantly. Spread the almonds on a baking sheet to cool. Combine the romaine, leafy green lettuce, green onion tops, mandarin oranges and caramelized almonds in a large bowl. Add the dressing and toss to coat.

Yield: 6 servings

Fabulous Group Salad

Salad

1/2 cup (1 stick) butter
2 tablespoons sugar
2 tablespoons brown sugar
1 1/2 cups pecan halves
1 head red leaf lettuce, torn into bite-size pieces
1 head green leaf lettuce, torn into bite-size pieces
1 head iceberg lettuce, torn into bite-size pieces
2 heads romaine, torn into bite-size pieces
1 red onion, very thinly sliced
1 cup seedless red grapes
2 avocados, peeled, pitted and cut into chunks
1 (4-ounce) package crumbled feta cheese

Dressing

1 envelope ranch salad dressing mix
1 cup mayonnaise
1 cup milk
2/3 cup blush wine vinaigrette dressing

For the salad, melt the butter in a saucepan. Add the sugar, brown sugar and pecans. Sauté for 5 minutes. Spread on waxed paper and let cool. Break into pieces. Combine the red leaf lettuce, green leaf lettuce, iceberg lettuce, romaine, onion, grapes, avocados, cheese and caramelized pecans in a large bowl. Toss to mix.

For the dressing, whisk the salad dressing mix, mayonnaise and milk in a bowl until blended. Remove 1/3 cup to a small bowl and reserve the remainder for another use. Add the vinaigrette dressing to the 1/3 cup ranch dressing and whisk until blended. Add to the salad and toss to coat.

Yield: 8 servings

Strawberry Spinach Salad

1 to 2 pints strawberries, sliced
1/3 cup slivered almonds, lightly toasted
2 (5-ounce) bags fresh spinach, rinsed and stems removed
1/4 cup vinegar
1/2 cup each vegetable oil and sugar
2 tablespoons sesame seeds
1 tablespoon poppy seeds
1 1/2 teaspoons finely chopped onion
1/4 teaspoon each Worcestershire sauce and paprika

Toss the strawberries, almonds and spinach in a large bowl. Whisk the remaining ingredients in a bowl until blended. Add to the salad and toss to mix.

Yield: 12 servings

Fresh Spinach Salad

1/4 cup sugar
1 teaspoon each salt and dry mustard
2 teaspoons poppy seeds
1 tablespoon onion juice
1/3 cup cider vinegar
1 cup vegetable oil
3/4 cup small curd cottage cheese
32 ounces fresh spinach, rinsed well and stems removed
8 ounces bacon, cooked and crumbled
2 hard-cooked eggs, chopped
8 ounces fresh mushrooms, sliced

Whisk the sugar, salt, dry mustard, poppy seeds, onion juice, vinegar, oil and cottage cheese in a bowl until well mixed. Cover and chill overnight. Combine the spinach, bacon, eggs and mushrooms in a large bowl. Toss to mix. Add the chilled dressing and toss to coat.

Yield: 8 servings

Black Bean Salad

2 (15-ounce) cans black beans, rinsed and drained
1 (11-ounce) can Shoe Peg corn, drained
1/2 bunch green onions, sliced
1/3 bunch cilantro, chopped
4 Roma tomatoes, chopped
Juice of 4 limes
1/2 cup light olive oil
Salt and pepper to taste

Combine the black beans, corn, green onions, cilantro, tomatoes, lime juice and olive oil in a bowl. Stir to mix well. Season with salt and pepper. Cover and chill for at least 8 hours. Serve as a salad or with tortilla chips as an appetizer.

Yield: 4 to 6 salad servings

Broccoli Slaw

2 (3-ounce) packages beef-flavor ramen noodles
1/2 cup sugar
1/3 cup vegetable oil
1/2 cup cider vinegar
1 (16-ounce) bag broccoli slaw
1 bunch green onions, chopped
1 cup salted sunflower seeds
1 (2-ounce) package slivered almonds

Combine the contents of the seasoning packets from the ramen noodles, sugar, oil and vinegar in a jar with a tight-fitting lid. Shake until well mixed. Chill for at least 4 hours. Combine the broccoli slaw, green onions, sunflower seeds, almonds and crumbled ramen noodles in a large bowl. Toss to mix. Add the chilled dressing and toss to coat.

Yield: 8 servings

Mom's Potato Salad

2 cups mayonnaise-type salad dressing
1/3 cup prepared mustard
1/4 cup cider vinegar
4 1/2 teaspoons sour cream
6 large kosher dill pickles, finely chopped
3 yellow onions, finely chopped
6 large unpeeled red-skinned potatoes
8 hard-cooked eggs, chopped
1 cup chopped celery
Salt and pepper to taste
Chopped fresh parsley
Paprika

Combine the salad dressing, mustard, vinegar, sour cream, pickles and onions in a large bowl. Stir to mix well. Cover and chill for several hours. Cook the potatoes in a saucepan of boiling salted water until firm but tender. Peel and cut into cubes. Add to the dressing and toss to coat. Add the chopped eggs and celery and toss to mix. Season with salt and pepper. Sprinkle with chopped parsley and paprika.

Yield: 8 servings

The Lord your God has blessed you in all the work of your hands.
Deuteronomy 2:7

Thanksgiving Cranberry Mold

1 (3-ounce) package cherry gelatin
1 envelope unflavored gelatin
1/2 cup boiling water
3/4 cup sugar
1 tablespoon lemon juice
1 cup canned pineapple juice
1 cup ground fresh cranberries
1 seedless orange with peel, ground
1 (8-ounce) can crushed pineapple, drained
1 cup chopped celery
1/2 cup chopped pecans

Dissolve the cherry gelatin and unflavored gelatin in the boiling water in a large bowl. Add the sugar, lemon juice and pineapple juice and stir until the sugar dissolves. Add the cranberries, orange, pineapple, celery and pecans. Stir to mix well. Pour into an oiled 10-inch ring mold. Chill until firm. Unmold onto a serving plate.

Yield: 10 servings

Congealed Orange Salad

1 (3-ounce) package orange gelatin
1/3 cup sugar
1 cup boiling water
1 cup sour cream
1 (8-ounce) can crushed pineapple, undrained
1 (6-ounce) can mandarin oranges, drained

Dissolve the orange gelatin and sugar in the boiling water in a bowl. Beat with an electric mixer until frothy. Add the sour cream and mix well. Stir in the pineapple and mandarin oranges. Pour into an 8-inch square baking dish. Chill overnight or until set.

Yield: 9 servings

Bow Tie Pasta and Grilled Chicken Salad

8 ounces bow tie pasta, cooked al dente and drained
1/2 green bell pepper, chopped
1/2 red bell pepper, chopped
1/3 cup crumbled feta cheese
1 rib celery, thinly sliced
12 kalamata olives, pitted and quartered
1/2 teaspoon salt
1/2 teaspoon pepper
1/4 cup (or more) Pasta Salad Dressing (below)
4 chicken breasts, grilled and sliced

Combine the pasta, green bell pepper, red bell pepper, cheese, celery, olives, salt, pepper and Pasta Salad Dressing in a large bowl. Toss to coat. Add more dressing if desired. Add the chicken and toss to mix. Cover and chill for at least 2 hours.

Yield: 8 servings

Pasta Salad Dressing

1/4 cup balsamic vinegar
1/4 cup vegetable oil
1/4 cup olive oil
1 tablespoon chopped fresh parsley
1 green onion, thinly sliced
1 garlic clove, minced
1 teaspoon lemon juice
1/2 teaspoon dried basil
1/2 teaspoon dried tarragon
1/4 teaspoon salt

Whisk the vinegar, vegetable oil, olive oil, parsley, green onion, garlic, lemon juice, basil, tarragon and salt in a small bowl until blended.

Yield: 1 cup

Chicken Salad Supreme

$2\frac{1}{2}$ cups chopped cooked chicken
1 cup finely chopped celery
1 cup sliced seedless green grapes
$\frac{1}{2}$ cup slivered almonds, toasted
2 tablespoons finely chopped fresh parsley
1 teaspoon salt
1 cup mayonnaise
$\frac{1}{2}$ cup whipping cream, whipped
Lettuce cups

Combine the chicken, celery, grapes, almonds, parsley, salt, mayonnaise and whipped cream in a large bowl. Stir gently to mix. Cover and chill for several hours or overnight. Serve in lettuce cups.

Yield: 8 servings

Abigail lost no time. She took two hundred loaves of bread, two skins of wine, five dressed sheep, five seahs of roasted grain, a hundred cakes of raisins and two hundred cakes of pressed figs, and loaded them on donkeys.
I Samuel 25:18

Chinese Chicken Salad

2 tablespoons sugar
1 teaspoon salt
1 teaspoon seasoned salt
1/2 teaspoon cracked pepper
1/4 cup vegetable oil
1 teaspoon sesame oil
3 tablespoons vinegar
4 chicken breasts, cooked and shredded
1 small head lettuce, shredded
3 green onions, chopped
2 tablespoons slivered almonds, toasted
1 tablespoon sesame seeds, toasted
1/2 cup chow mein noodles

Whisk the sugar, salt, seasoned salt, pepper, vegetable oil, sesame oil and vinegar in a large bowl until blended. Cover and chill. Add the chicken, lettuce, green onions, almonds, sesame seeds and chow mein noodles to the dressing. Toss to mix and serve immediately.

Yield: 4 servings

Mexican Chicken Salad

4 cups chopped cooked chicken
2 cups (8 ounces) shredded sharp Cheddar cheese
1 (16-ounce) can red kidney beans, rinsed and drained
1 onion, chopped
1/2 cup sliced black olives
2 tablespoons chopped red bell pepper
2 tablespoons chopped green bell pepper
1 (4-ounce) can chopped green chiles, drained
1 envelope taco seasoning mix
1/2 cup sour cream
1/2 cup mayonnaise
2 avocados, peeled, pitted and chopped
Shredded lettuce
2 tomatoes, chopped
Corn chips

Combine the chicken, cheese, kidney beans, onion, olives, red bell pepper, green bell pepper and green chiles in a large bowl. Toss to mix. Stir the taco seasoning mix, sour cream and mayonnaise in a small bowl until blended. Add to the chicken mixture and stir to mix well. Cover and chill. Fold in the avocados just before serving. Arrange shredded lettuce on 12 salad plates. Mound the chicken salad on the lettuce. Top each with chopped tomatoes and corn chips.

Yield: 12 servings

Shrimp Salad

1 garlic clove, cut
$1^{1}/_{2}$ pounds large shrimp, cooked, peeled, deveined and chopped
Few drops of lemon juice
1 cup finely chopped celery
$^{1}/_{2}$ cup chopped green onions
$^{1}/_{4}$ cup chopped fresh parsley
1 cup mayonnaise
$^{1}/_{2}$ teaspoon dill weed
Freshly ground black pepper to taste
Cayenne pepper to taste
Salt to taste
4 avocado shells or tomato shells
Chopped fresh parsley

Rub a salad bowl with the cut garlic clove. Discard the garlic. Add the shrimp to the bowl and sprinkle with lemon juice. Add the celery, green onions, $^{1}/_{4}$ cup parsley, mayonnaise, and dill weed. Season with black pepper, cayenne pepper and salt. Toss to mix. Cover and chill for 8 hours. Serve in avocado shells and top with chopped parsley.

Yield: 4 servings

This is my commandment, that ye love one another, as I have loved you.

John 15:12

The women of our church have felt called to share God's love with those beyond the church family, touching the lives of people within their community, their city, and their world. Early in our history, ladies gathered at the church to roll bandages and make bed linens to send to missionary hospitals in Africa. Later, Mary Anderson organized a group of women to visit and care for out-of-town patients and their family members at Baylor Hospital. Today, Jewell Cantrell, Claudia O'Conner, and others still meet and spend time mending clothes for residents of nursing homes in the community.

Jesus said, *By this all men will know that you are my disciples, if you love one another* (John 13:35). Our community, our city, and our world have been shown God's love by women who have chosen to be his disciples and obey the command to love one another.

Vegetables and Side Dishes

Corn Pudding

1/4 cup sugar
3 tablespoons flour
2 teaspoons baking powder
2 teaspoons salt
6 eggs
2 cups heavy cream
1/2 cup (1 stick) butter, melted
6 cups frozen whole kernel corn

Mix the sugar, flour, baking powder and salt in a bowl. Beat the eggs in a large bowl. Stir in the cream and melted butter. Add the dry ingredients gradually, stirring until smooth. Add the frozen corn and stir to mix. Pour into a lightly greased 9×13-inch baking dish. Bake at 350 degrees for 45 minutes or until the top is deep golden brown.

Yield: 15 servings

Mother's Fresh Creamed Corn

6 ears of corn
1/2 cup flour
2 cups milk
1/2 cup sugar
1/4 teaspoon salt
1/4 cup (1/2 stick) butter

Cut the kernels from the cobs into a medium saucepan. Scrape off the remaining pulp and juice with a knife and add to the corn kernels. Stir in the flour. Add the milk, sugar, salt and butter. Cook over low heat until the desired thickness is reached, stirring frequently.

Yield: 8 servings

Skillet Fried Corn

12 ears of corn
8 slices bacon
1/2 cup (1 stick) butter or margarine
2 to 4 tablespoons sugar
2 teaspoons salt
1/2 teaspoon pepper

Cut the kernels from the cobs into a large bowl. Scrape off the remaining pulp and juice with a knife and add to the corn kernels. Cook the bacon in a large skillet until crisp. Remove to paper towels to drain; crumble. Remove all but 1/4 cup of the bacon drippings from the skillet. Add the corn, butter, sugar, salt and pepper to the skillet. Cook over medium heat for 20 minutes, stirring frequently. Spoon into a serving dish and top with the crumbled bacon.

Yield: 12 servings

Shoe Peg Corn Casserole

1/4 cup (1/2 stick) butter
1/4 cup milk
8 ounces cream cheese
2 (14-ounce) cans Shoe Peg corn, drained
1 (4-ounce) can chopped green chiles
Salt and pepper to taste

Melt the butter in a saucepan. Add the milk and cream cheese. Cook until the cream cheese melts, stirring frequently. Remove from the heat and stir in the corn and green chiles. Season with salt and pepper. Pour into a greased 2-quart baking dish. Bake, covered, at 350 degrees for 30 minutes.

Yield: 6 servings

Zucchini and Corn Con Chile Verde

1 scant tablespoon olive oil
1/4 cup chopped red onion
1 teaspoon minced garlic (about 1 clove)
4 to 6 baby zucchini, sliced (about 1 pound)
1 (10-ounce) package frozen white Shoe Peg corn, thawed
Freshly ground pepper to taste
1 (4-ounce) can chopped green chiles
1/2 cup (2 ounces) shredded Monterey Jack cheese

Heat the olive oil in a large skillet. Add the onion and garlic and sauté until tender. Add the zucchini and corn and cook until light brown. Sprinkle with pepper. Stir in the green chiles. Cook until heated through, stirring constantly. Sprinkle with the cheese.

Yield: 8 servings

Note: You may substitute 1 (14-ounce) can white Shoe Peg corn, drained, for the frozen corn.

This bread of ours was warm when we
packed it at home on the day we left to come to you.
Joshua 9:12

Asparagus Soufflé

1 cup herb-seasoned stuffing mix
1 (10-ounce) can cream of asparagus soup
1 tablespoon lemon juice
1 (10-ounce) package frozen asparagus, chopped and thawed
4 egg yolks, beaten
4 egg whites
1/4 teaspoon cream of tartar

Stir the stuffing mix, soup and lemon juice in a bowl. Add the asparagus and egg yolks and stir to mix well. Beat the egg whites and cream of tartar in a mixing bowl until stiff peaks form. Fold into the asparagus mixture. Pour into a greased 1 1/2-quart soufflé or baking dish. Bake at 325 degrees for 1 1/2 hours.
Serve immediately.

Yield: 4 servings

At mealtime Boaz said to her, "Come over here.
Have some bread and dip it in the wine vinegar."
Ruth 2:14

Broccoli with Horseradish Sauce

$^1/_4$ cup ($^1/_2$ stick) butter, melted
$^3/_4$ cup mayonnaise
1 tablespoon prepared horseradish
1 tablespoon grated onion
$^1/_4$ teaspoon salt
$^1/_4$ teaspoon dry mustard
Dash of cayenne pepper
Broccoli, cooked tender-crisp

Pour the melted butter into a small bowl and let cool slightly. Add the mayonnaise, horseradish, onion, salt, dry mustard and cayenne pepper. Stir to mix well. Cover and chill for at least 1 hour. Spoon over hot cooked broccoli.

Yield: 4 to 6 servings

Elegant Broccoli and Walnuts

1 pound bacon
1 cup chopped walnuts
$^3/_4$ cup sliced green onions
$1^1/_2$ to 2 pounds fresh broccoli, cut into short spears or florets and cooked tender-crisp

Cook the bacon in a large skillet until crisp. Remove to paper towels to drain; crumble. Remove all but 1 tablespoon of the bacon drippings from the skillet. Add the walnuts to the skillet. Cook over medium heat for 3 to 5 minutes, stirring constantly. Add the green onions and cook for 3 minutes, stirring constantly. Arrange the hot broccoli on a serving platter. Spoon the walnut mixture over the top and sprinkle with the crumbled bacon.

Yield: 6 to 8 servings

Green Beans with Caramelized Onions

2 sweet onions, thinly sliced and slices halved
2 tablespoons butter or margarine
2 tablespoons brown sugar
1 pound fresh green beans, cooked tender-crisp
1 to 2 teaspoons balsamic vinegar (optional)

Place the onions in a nonstick skillet. Cook over medium-high heat for 8 to 10 minutes without stirring. Cook for 5 to 10 minutes longer or until golden brown, stirring frequently. Reduce the heat to medium and stir in the butter and brown sugar. Add the green beans. Cook for 5 minutes or until heated through, stirring frequently. Add the vinegar and toss to mix.

Yield: 6 servings

Honey-Glazed Baby Carrots

2 tablespoons unsalted butter
2 tablespoons honey
1 pound baby carrots, cooked tender-crisp
Salt and pepper to taste

Combine the butter and honey in a small skillet. Cook over low heat until the butter melts. Add the carrots. Season with salt and pepper. Cook for 1 minute or until the carrots are well coated, stirring constantly.

Yield: 4 to 6 servings

Onion Bake

6 onions, thinly sliced (about 2 pounds)
2 tablespoons butter
Salt and pepper to taste
35 butter crackers, crumbled
8 ounces Cheddar cheese, shredded
1 (4-ounce) can chopped green chiles (optional)

Place the onion slices in a large saucepan and cover with water. Bring to a boil. Remove from the heat and drain. Repeat 2 more times. Drain the onions in a colander until dry. Melt the butter in a saucepan. Add the onions and season with salt and pepper. Sauté over medium heat until tender. Spread the onions in a buttered $1^1/_2$-quart baking dish. Top with the cracker crumbs and sprinkle with the cheese. Top with the green chiles. Bake, covered, at 325 degrees for 30 minutes.

Yield: 8 servings

If you come with us, we will share with
you whatever good things the Lord gives us.
Numbers 10:32

Roasted Potato Trio

$1/4$ cup ($1/2$ stick) butter
$1/4$ cup olive oil
$1/3$ cup chopped fresh rosemary
$2\,1/2$ pounds sweet potatoes, peeled and cut into $1/2$-inch slices
2 pounds red-skinned potatoes, peeled and cut into $1/2$-inch slices
1 pound Yukon Gold potatoes, peeled and cut into $1/2$-inch slices
$1/2$ teaspoon salt
$1/2$ teaspoon freshly ground pepper

Combine the butter, olive oil and rosemary in a small saucepan. Cook over medium heat until the butter melts, stirring constantly. Brush half the butter mixture on 2 baking sheets. Arrange the sweet potato, red-skinned potato and Yukon Gold potato slices in a single layer on the prepared sheets. Brush with the remaining butter mixture. Sprinkle with the salt and pepper. Bake at 450 degrees for 35 minutes or until tender and golden brown.

Yield: 12 servings

Cheese Potatoes

1 cup sour cream
2 teaspoons salt
2 cups cottage cheese
$1/4$ cup finely chopped green onions
1 garlic clove, minced
5 cups peeled, cooked and cubed potatoes
Shredded American cheese to taste
Paprika

Mix the sour cream, salt, cottage cheese, green onions and garlic in a bowl. Fold in the cooked potatoes. Spoon into a greased baking dish. Top with American cheese and sprinkle with paprika. Bake at 350 degrees for 40 to 45 minutes or until hot and bubbly.

Yield: 8 servings

Spinach Madeleine

2 (10-ounce) packages frozen chopped spinach
1/4 cup (1/2 stick) butter
2 tablespoons chopped onion
2 tablespoons flour
1/2 cup milk
1/2 teaspoon pepper
3/4 teaspoon celery salt
3/4 teaspoon garlic salt
1/2 teaspoon salt
6 ounces Velveeta jalapeño cheese, cubed
Bread crumbs (optional)

Cook the spinach according to the package directions. Drain and reserve 1/2 cup of the liquid. Melt the butter in a large saucepan. Add the onion and sauté until tender. Stir in the flour gradually. Cook until bubbly, stirring constantly. Add the milk and reserved cooking liquid. Cook until thickened, stirring constantly. Add the pepper, celery salt, garlic salt, salt and Velveeta. Cook until the Velveeta melts, stirring constantly. Add the spinach and mix well. Top with bread crumbs and serve.

Yield: 6 servings

Note: The flavor is best if made 1 day ahead. Cover and chill. Reheat before serving.

Spinach-Stuffed Squash

5 1/3 tablespoons butter
2 (10-ounce) packages frozen chopped spinach, cooked, drained and squeezed dry
3 ounces light cream cheese
1 teaspoon garlic salt
1/2 teaspoon black pepper
1/8 teaspoon cayenne pepper
4 large yellow squash, cooked, halved lengthwise and seeded
1/4 cup (1 ounce) grated Parmesan cheese
2 tablespoons bread crumbs

Melt the butter in a large skillet. Stir in the spinach. Add the cream cheese, garlic salt, black pepper and cayenne pepper. Cook until the cream cheese melts, stirring constantly. Arrange the squash halves in a lightly greased 9×13-inch baking dish. Spoon the spinach filling into the squash shells. Sprinkle with the Parmesan cheese and bread crumbs. Bake at 400 degrees for 20 minutes.

Yield: 8 servings

Calabacitas (Squash Casserole)

2 tablespoons vegetable oil
1 onion, chopped
1 garlic clove, minced
2 yellow squash, cut into 1-inch cubes
2 zucchini, cut into 1-inch cubes
1 cup green chiles, seeded and chopped
2 cups fresh corn kernels
10 corn tortillas
2 cups (8 ounces) shredded Monterey Jack or Cheddar cheese
1 (10-ounce) can cream of chicken soup

Heat the oil in a large skillet. Add the onion, garlic, yellow squash and zucchini. Sauté until the vegetables are tender-crisp. Stir in the green chiles and corn. Spread 1/3 of the squash mixture in the bottom of a greased 9×13-inch baking dish. Cover with 3 1/3 tortillas and sprinkle with 1/2 cup cheese. Repeat the layers 2 more times. Spread the soup on top and sprinkle with the remaining 1/2 cup cheese. Bake at 325 degrees for 30 minutes. Serve with fresh green tomatoes.

Yield: 8 servings

Squash Casserole

1 pound summer squash, sliced
1 onion, chopped
1/3 cup water
1/4 teaspoon salt
1/4 cup (1/2 stick) butter
2 eggs, beaten
1/2 cup (2 ounces) shredded Cheddar cheese
1/4 cup cracker crumbs
1 tablespoon sugar
1/4 teaspoon soy sauce
1/8 teaspoon pepper
1/4 cup (1 ounce) shredded Cheddar cheese
1/4 cup cracker crumbs
1/8 teaspoon paprika

Combine the squash, onion, water and salt in a saucepan. Cook until the vegetables are tender; drain. Mash the squash in a bowl. Add the butter, eggs, 1/2 cup cheese, 1/4 cup cracker crumbs, sugar, soy sauce and pepper. Stir to mix well. Pour into a greased 1 1/2-quart baking dish. Bake at 350 degrees for 20 minutes. Top with 1/4 cup cheese and 1/4 cup cracker crumbs. Sprinkle with the paprika. Bake for 10 to 15 minutes longer.

Yield: 4 servings

Holiday Sweet Potatoes

Potatoes

4 or 5 sweet potatoes, peeled and boiled until tender
1/4 to 1/2 cup milk
1/2 cup (1 stick) butter, softened
1/2 cup sugar
Cinnamon to taste
Salt to taste

Glaze

1/2 cup (1 stick) butter
1/2 cup sugar
1/2 cup half-and-half
1 teaspoon vanilla extract

For the potatoes, mash the sweet potatoes in a large bowl. Add the milk, butter and sugar and beat until smooth. Season with cinnamon and salt. Spread in a greased 9×13-inch baking dish.

For the glaze, combine the butter and sugar in a large heavy skillet. Cook until caramelized, stirring constantly. Do not allow to burn. Stir in the half-and-half gradually. Stir in the vanilla. Pour evenly over the sweet potato mixture. Bake at 350 degrees for 30 to 40 minutes or until bubbly.

Yield: 12 servings

Note: You may mix part or all of the glaze into the potatoes instead of spreading it on top. Marshmallows may be added on top near the end of baking.

Sweet Potato Casserole

3 cups mashed cooked sweet potatoes
1 cup sugar
1/2 cup evaporated milk
5 1/3 tablespoons butter, softened
2 eggs, beaten
1 teaspoon vanilla extract
1 cup flaked coconut
1 cup pecans, chopped
1 cup packed brown sugar
1/3 cup flour
5 1/3 tablespoons butter, melted

Combine the mashed sweet potatoes, sugar, evaporated milk, softened butter, eggs and vanilla in a large bowl. Stir to mix well. Pour into a shallow baking dish. Combine the coconut, pecans, brown sugar, flour and melted butter in a bowl. Stir to mix well. Sprinkle on top of the sweet potato mixture. Bake at 350 degrees for 20 to 30 minutes.

Yield: 6 servings

Note: This may be prepared ahead. Cover and chill before baking.

Sour Cream Cheese Rice

6 cups cooked white rice
1/2 cup (1 stick) butter, melted
1 (10-ounce) can cream of chicken soup
12 ounces Velveeta cheese, shredded
2 cups sour cream
1 teaspoon salt
1/2 small onion, chopped
1 cup crushed cornflakes
1/4 cup (1/2 stick) butter, melted

Combine the cooked rice, 1/2 cup melted butter, soup, Velveeta, sour cream, salt and onion in a large bowl. Stir to mix well. Pour into a 3-quart baking dish. Sprinkle with the cornflake crumbs and drizzle with 1/4 cup melted butter. Bake at 325 degrees for 30 minutes or until bubbly.

Yield: 12 servings

Now then, what do you have on hand?
Give me five loaves of bread, or whatever you can find.
I Samuel 21:3

Nutty Wild Rice

1 cup wild rice
2 cups chicken broth
2 tablespoons butter
1 cup brown rice
$2^2/_3$ cups chicken broth
2 tablespoons butter
3 tablespoons butter
4 shallots, minced
4 ounces mushrooms, sliced
Salt and pepper to taste
1 cup pecans
$^1/_2$ cup chopped fresh parsley

Combine the wild rice, 2 cups chicken broth and 2 tablespoons butter in a saucepan. Cook, covered, over low heat for 1 hour or until all the liquid is absorbed. Combine the brown rice, $2^2/_3$ cups chicken broth and 2 tablespoons butter in a saucepan. Bring to a boil and reduce the heat. Cook, covered, over low heat for 50 minutes or until all the liquid is absorbed. Melt 3 tablespoons butter in a large skillet. Add the shallots and mushrooms. Sauté for 5 minutes. Remove from the heat and add the wild rice and brown rice. Toss to mix. Season with salt and pepper. Add the pecans and parsley and toss to mix.

Yield: 12 servings

Marinated Tomatoes

6 large tomatoes, peeled
1/4 cup thinly sliced scallions (white and green parts)
1/4 cup finely chopped fresh parsley
1 garlic clove, minced
2 tablespoons chopped fresh thyme leaves, or
1/2 teaspoon dried thyme
1 teaspoon salt
1/4 teaspoon freshly ground pepper
2/3 cup vegetable oil
1/4 cup red or white wine vinegar

Cut the tomatoes into thick slices and arrange in a shallow dish. Mix the scallions, parsley, garlic, thyme, salt and pepper in a small bowl. Sprinkle over the tomatoes. Combine the oil and vinegar in a jar with a tight-fitting lid. Shake until well mixed. Pour over the tomatoes. Cover and chill for several hours or overnight, spooning the dressing over the tomatoes occasionally. Drain the excess dressing before serving.

Yield: 6 to 8 servings

Charleston Cheese Grits

4 1/2 cups water
1 cup quick-cooking grits
1 teaspoon salt
1/2 cup (1 stick) butter
2 (6-ounce) packages processed garlic cheese
Dash of Tabasco sauce
Dash of Worcestershire sauce
2 eggs
Milk
1 cup cornflakes

Bring the water to a boil in a saucepan. Add the grits, salt and butter. Cook, covered, for 5 minutes or until thickened, stirring occasionally. Add the garlic cheese, Tabasco sauce and Worcestershire sauce. Cook until the cheese melts, stirring constantly. Remove from the heat. Beat the eggs in a 1-cup measuring cup. Add enough milk to make 1 cup. Stir into the grits mixture. Pour into a greased 9×13-inch baking dish. Top with the cornflakes. Bake at 400 degrees for 1 hour or until set.

Yield: 8 servings

Baked Macaroni and Cheese

6 tablespoons butter or margarine
6 tablespoons flour
4 cups milk
3 cups (12 ounces) shredded sharp Cheddar cheese
1 cup (4 ounces) grated Parmesan cheese
Salt and pepper to taste
16 ounces medium shell or penne pasta, cooked al dente and drained
1/3 cup grated Parmesan cheese

Melt the butter in a saucepan. Add the flour and cook until smooth, stirring constantly. Add the milk and cook over medium heat until thickened, stirring constantly. Add the Cheddar cheese and 1 cup Parmesan cheese. Cook until the cheese melts, stirring frequently. Season with salt and pepper. Place the cooked pasta in a lightly greased baking dish. Pour the sauce over the pasta. Sprinkle with 1/3 cup Parmesan cheese. Bake at 350 degrees for 30 minutes or until bubbly and light brown.

Yield: 12 servings

Cinnamon Candied Apples

1 cup sugar
2 cups water
1 cup red hot cinnamon candies
6 to 8 small firm apples, such as Jonathan, cored

Combine the sugar, water and candies in a large deep saucepan. Bring to a boil. Simmer until the candies dissolve. Peel the apples. Place the apples gradually into the boiling syrup so that the liquid continues to boil. Cook until the apples are tender but not mushy, turning frequently Remove with a slotted spoon to a wire rack to cool.

Yield: 6 to 8 servings

So he went and got them and brought them to his mother,
and she prepared some tasty food, just the way his father liked it.
Genesis 27:14

Cranberry Chutney

16 ounces fresh or frozen cranberries
1 apple, peeled, cored and chopped
2 cups packed brown sugar
$^{1}/_{4}$ cup white vinegar
$^{1}/_{2}$ teaspoon salt
$^{1}/_{4}$ teaspoon ginger
$^{1}/_{4}$ teaspoon cloves
$^{1}/_{4}$ teaspoon allspice
$^{1}/_{4}$ teaspoon dry mustard

Combine the cranberries, apple, brown sugar, vinegar, salt, ginger, cloves, allspice and dry mustard in a large heavy saucepan. Bring to a boil, stirring constantly. Reduce the heat and simmer until thick, stirring frequently. Remove to a bowl. Cover and chill until ready to serve.

Yield: 3 cups

The cheerful heart has a continual feast.
Proverbs 15:15

Cranberry Apple Crunch

4 cups chopped peeled Granny Smith apples
2 cups fresh cranberries
$1^1/_2$ teaspoons lemon juice
1 cup sugar
$1^1/_3$ cups quick-cooking oats
1 cup walnuts, chopped
$^1/_2$ cup packed brown sugar
$^1/_2$ cup (1 stick) butter, melted

Mix the apples and cranberries in a bowl. Spread in a lightly greased 9×13-inch baking dish. Sprinkle with the lemon juice. Top with the sugar. Mix the oats, walnuts, brown sugar and melted butter in a bowl until moistened and crumbly. Sprinkle over the fruit. Bake at 325 degrees for 1 hour or 350 degrees for 45 minutes. Remove to a wire rack to cool. Good with pork tenderloin.

Yield: 12 servings

Note: May also be served as a dessert with ice cream.

Then all the people went away to eat and drink, to send portions of food and to celebrate with joy because they now understood the words that had been made known to them.
Nehemiah 8:12

Peace I leave with you, let not your heart be troubled neither let it be afraid.

John 14:27

In the early 1940s, the church met in a remodeled home on Lovers Lane. Christine Wallace taught the Homemakers Class of over one hundred women each Sunday. While the women enjoyed a Bible lesson and each other's company, their children were taught and cared for in the church nursery. The nursery has always played an important role, not only in the Christian education of our children, but also as a place where mothers could leave their young ones with confidence and peace of mind. The children learned that church was a safe place where they would be loved by leaders like Louise Houghton, Edna Wilson, and Myra Nichols.

The church remains a place where women and their children can come to find friends and fellowship, returning home with the peace that comes from having spent time with the Lord.

Entrées

Flank Steak Marinade

$^3/_4$ cup olive oil
$^1/_3$ cup soy sauce
$^1/_4$ cup red wine vinegar
$^1/_4$ cup lemon juice
2 tablespoons Worcestershire sauce
1 tablespoon dry mustard
2 teaspoons salt
$1^1/_2$ teaspoons pepper
1 teaspoon dried parsley flakes
$^1/_4$ teaspoon garlic powder
2 (1-pound) flank steaks

Process the olive oil, soy sauce, vinegar, lemon juice, Worcestershire sauce, dry mustard, salt, pepper, parsley and garlic powder in a blender until well mixed. Pour over the steaks in a shallow dish. Cover and chill overnight. Remove the steaks from the marinade and discard the marinade. Grill over hot coals for 7 minutes per side or to desired doneness.

Yield: 8 servings

Estofado

3 pounds sirloin steak, cut into 2-inch strips
3 tablespoons olive oil or bacon drippings
2 large onions, chopped
2 large green bell peppers, cut into strips
2 (14-ounce) cans stewed tomatoes
2 bay leaves
2 teaspoons fines herbes
1 teaspoon ground ginger
3 to 4 tablespoons soy sauce
Salt and pepper to taste
6 cups hot cooked rice

Brown the sirloin in the olive oil in a large skillet. Add the onions and bell peppers and sauté until the vegetables are tender-crisp. Stir in the tomatoes, bay leaves, fines herbes, ginger and soy sauce. Season with salt and pepper. Cook over low heat until the sirloin is tender. Remove the bay leaves. Serve over the rice.

Yield: 8 servings

The Best Barbecued Ribs

1/2 cup (1 stick) butter
3/4 cup ketchup
1/2 cup packed brown sugar
3 tablespoons lemon juice
1 tablespoon Dijon mustard
2 teaspoons steak sauce
2 teaspoons hot pepper sauce
2 teaspoons Worcestershire sauce
4 pounds baby back ribs, lightly salted

Melt the butter in a saucepan. Stir in the ketchup, brown sugar, lemon juice, Dijon mustard, steak sauce, hot pepper sauce and Worcestershire sauce. Cook until the sugar is melted, stirring frequently. Keep warm. Place the ribs on a rack in a roasting pan. Spread with some of the sauce. Bake at 325 degrees for 30 minutes. Baste with the sauce. Bake for 2 hours longer or until cooked through and tender, brushing with the remaining sauce every 15 minutes.

Yield: 4 servings

Special Beef Tenderloin

1/2 cup Worcestershire sauce
1/2 cup teriyaki sauce
1 tablespoon freshly cracked pepper
1 (6- to 8-pound) beef tenderloin

Combine the Worcestershire sauce, teriyaki sauce and pepper in a sealable plastic bag. Add the tenderloin and seal the bag tightly. Marinate in the refrigerator for 6 hours. Remove the tenderloin to a rack in a roasting pan. Discard the marinade. Roast at 400 degrees for 40 minutes for medium-rare.

Yield: 12 to 16 servings

Rigatoni with Sirloin and Gorgonzola Sauce

1 tablespoon olive oil
1 pound sirloin steak, cut into cubes
1/4 teaspoon salt
1/4 teaspoon pepper
1 tablespoon olive oil
8 ounces portobello mushrooms, stems removed, caps cut into halves and sliced
1/4 teaspoon salt
1 shallot, minced
3/4 cup chicken broth
1/4 teaspoon Worcestershire sauce
4 ounces Gorgonzola cheese, crumbled
1/2 cup heavy cream
1 teaspoon salt
1/2 teaspoon pepper
1 tablespoon chopped fresh parsley
12 ounces rigatoni pasta, cooked al dente and drained

Heat 1 tablespoon olive oil in a large skillet over medium heat. Season the steak cubes with 1/4 teaspoon salt and 1/4 teaspoon pepper. Add to the hot oil and sauté for 8 minutes or until brown on all sides. Remove the steak to a bowl and keep warm. Heat 1 tablespoon olive oil in the skillet. Add the mushrooms and 1/4 teaspoon salt and sauté for 2 minutes. Remove from the pan and place in the bowl with the steak. Add the shallot, chicken broth and Worcestershire sauce to the hot skillet. Cook, stirring up any browned bits, to deglaze the pan. Simmer for 5 minutes or until the liquid is reduced to 1/3 cup. Add the steak and mushrooms with any juices, the cheese, cream, 1 teaspoon salt, 1/2 teaspoon pepper and parsley. Cook for 1 minute, stirring constantly. Pour over the hot pasta in a large bowl and toss to coat. Serve immediately.

Yield: 4 to 6 servings

Company Casserole

1 tablespoon butter
1 pound ground beef
1 (8-ounce) can tomato sauce
1 cup cottage cheese
1 cup sour cream
8 ounces cream cheese, softened
$1/3$ cup chopped onion
$1/3$ cup chopped bell pepper
8 ounces egg noodles, cooked al dente and drained
2 tablespoons butter, melted

Melt 1 tablespoon butter in a skillet. Brown the ground beef in the butter, stirring until crumbly; drain. Stir in the tomato sauce and remove from the heat. Combine the cottage cheese, sour cream, cream cheese, onion and bell pepper in a bowl. Stir to mix well. Spread $1/2$ of the noodles in a buttered 9×13-inch baking dish. Spread with the cheese mixture. Top with the remaining noodles. Pour the melted butter over the noodles. Spoon the tomato mixture evenly over the top. Bake at 350 degrees for 20 to 30 minutes.

Yield: 12 servings

Dr. Pepper Meat Loaf

$1^1/_2$ pounds ground beef
2 eggs
$1^1/_2$ cups bread crumbs
1 (8-ounce) can tomato sauce
1 tablespoon dried onion flakes
1 teaspoon onion salt
$^1/_2$ teaspoon salt
$^1/_8$ teaspoon pepper
$^2/_3$ cup barbecue sauce
1 (8-ounce) can tomato sauce
1 tablespoon Worcestershire sauce
1 tablespoon prepared mustard
$^1/_3$ cup packed brown sugar
$^1/_4$ cup Dr. Pepper

Combine the ground beef, eggs, bread crumbs and 1 can tomato sauce in a bowl. Stir to mix well. Add the onion flakes, onion salt, salt and pepper and stir to mix well. Shape into a loaf and place in a deep 3-quart baking dish. Mix the barbecue sauce, 1 can tomato sauce, Worcestershire sauce, mustard, brown sugar and Dr. Pepper in a bowl. Pour half over the meat loaf. Bake, covered, at 350 degrees for 20 minutes. Pour the remaining sauce over the meat loaf. Bake, uncovered, for 45 minutes longer or until cooked through.

Yield: 8 servings

Wonderful Lasagna

1 pound hot Italian sausage, casings removed
8 ounces ground chuck
1/2 cup finely chopped green onions
2 or 3 garlic cloves, minced
3 to 4 tablespoons olive oil
1 (29-ounce) can tomato sauce
1 (6-ounce) can tomato paste
1/2 teaspoon each salt and freshly ground pepper
1/4 teaspoon dried oregano
Dash of dried basil
1 cup (4 ounces) shredded Monterey Jack cheese
1 cup each ricotta cheese and cottage cheese
1/2 cup each finely chopped green onions and finely chopped fresh parsley
1 egg, beaten
1/2 teaspoon each dried basil and dried marjoram
6 to 8 slices bacon, crisp-cooked and crumbled
1 (10-ounce) package frozen chopped spinach, thawed and drained well
1/2 cup (2 ounces) freshly grated Parmesan cheese
1/2 cup soft bread crumbs
1 egg yolk
2 tablespoons olive oil (optional)
5 lasagna noodles, cooked al dente and drained
1 cup (4 ounces) shredded Monterey Jack cheese
1 (8-ounce) package sliced Swiss cheese

Brown the sausage, ground chuck, 1/2 cup green onions and garlic in 3 to 4 tablespoons olive oil in a large skillet, stirring until the sausage and ground chuck are crumbly; drain. Stir in the tomato sauce, tomato paste, salt, pepper, oregano and dash of basil. Bring to a boil and reduce the heat. Simmer, covered, for 20 to 30 minutes, stirring frequently. Cover and chill for 8 hours.

Combine 1 cup Monterey Jack cheese, the ricotta cheese, cottage cheese, 1/2 cup green onions, parsley, egg, 1/2 teaspoon basil and marjoram in a bowl. Stir to mix well. Combine the bacon, spinach, Parmesan cheese, bread crumbs, egg yolk and 2 tablespoons olive oil in a bowl. Stir to mix well. Spread half the chilled meat sauce in a lightly greased 9×13-inch baking dish. Top with half the ricotta cheese mixture. Spread with half the spinach mixture. Arrange the noodles on top. Repeat the layers with the remaining meat sauce, ricotta cheese mixture and spinach mixture. Sprinkle with 1 cup Monterey Jack cheese. Top evenly with the Swiss cheese slices. Bake at 350 degrees for 40 to 45 minutes or until the cheese melts and the lasagna is hot and bubbly.

Yield: 12 servings

Lasagna

12 ounces ground beef
4 ounces sweet or mild Italian sausage, casings removed
1 garlic clove, minced
1 tablespoon basil
1½ teaspoons salt
16 ounces tomatoes, peeled and chopped (about 3 medium)
2 (6-ounce) cans tomato paste
3 cups cottage cheese
½ cup (2 ounces) grated Parmesan cheese
2 tablespoons chopped fresh parsley
2 eggs, beaten
1 teaspoon salt
½ teaspoon pepper
12 lasagna noodles, cooked al dente and drained
16 ounces mozzarella cheese, shredded

Brown the ground beef and sausage in a skillet, stirring until crumbly; drain. Stir in the garlic, basil, 1½ teaspoons salt, tomatoes and tomato paste. Simmer, uncovered, for 30 minutes. Mix the cottage cheese, Parmesan cheese, parsley, eggs, 1 teaspoon salt and pepper in a bowl. Arrange 6 lasagna noodles in a 9×13-inch baking dish. Spread with half the cottage cheese mixture. Sprinkle with half the mozzarella cheese and top with half the meat sauce. Repeat the layers. Bake at 375 degrees for 30 minutes.

Yield: 12 servings

Hot Ham Sandwiches

$1/2$ cup (1 stick) butter, softened
$1/3$ cup mayonnaise
$4\,1/2$ teaspoons Dijon mustard
$1/2$ teaspoon Worcestershire sauce
1 tablespoon poppy seeds
16 large or 32 small croissants
2 to 3 pounds very thinly sliced Black Forest ham
1 to 2 pounds thinly sliced Monterey Jack cheese with peppers

Combine the butter, mayonnaise, Dijon mustard, Worcestersshire sauce and poppy seeds in a bowl. Stir to mix well. Cut the croissants into halves. Spread the butter mixture on both halves of each croissant. Layer half the croissants with the ham and cheese. Top each with half a croissant. Wrap the sandwiches in foil and place on a baking sheet. Bake at 325 degrees for 30 minutes or until the cheese melts.

Yield: 16 servings

Ham Balls

2 pounds ground ham
1 pound ground pork
2 eggs, beaten
1 cup milk
1 cup bread crumbs
$1\,1/2$ cups packed brown sugar
$1/2$ cup each vinegar and water
1 tablespoon dry mustard

Combine the ham, pork, eggs, milk and bread crumbs in a bowl. Stir to mix well. Shape into 1-inch balls and arrange in a 9×13-inch baking pan. Mix the brown sugar, vinegar, water and dry mustard in a small saucepan. Heat to boiling, stirring often. Pour over the meatballs. Bake at 350 degrees for 45 to 50 minutes or until cooked through, basting occasionally.

Yield: 6 dozen meatballs

Apricot-Glazed Pork Tenderloin

2 (1-pound) pork tenderloins
Salt, pepper and seasoned salt to taste
1 (8-ounce) bottle Italian or oil and vinegar salad dressing
1 (12-ounce) jar apricot preserves

Rinse the pork tenderloins and pat dry. Season with salt, pepper and seasoned salt. Place in a shallow dish and pour the salad dressing over the tenderloins. Cover and chill for at least 8 hours, turning occasionally. Remove the tenderloins and discard the marinade. Place the tenderloins in a 9×13-inch baking dish lined with foil. Let stand for 10 minutes. Bake at 375 degrees for 20 to 30 minutes. Cover with foil and bake for 20 minutes longer. Spoon 1/2 to 3/4 of the apricot preserves over the tenderloins. Cover and bake for 20 to 25 minutes longer or until cooked through. Slice the tenderloins and top with the remaining preserves, if desired.

Yield: 8 servings

After he washed his face, he came out
and, controlling himself, said, "serve the food."
Genesis 43:31

Stuffed Pork Tenderloin

$^1/_2$ cup chopped dried apricots
$^1/_2$ cup boiling water
2 tablespoons butter or margarine
2 green onions, finely chopped
$^1/_2$ cup chopped fresh mushrooms
$^1/_4$ cup chopped green bell pepper
1 (6-ounce) package long grain and wild rice mix, cooked according to the package directions
3 tablespoons chopped pecans
1 tablespoon chopped fresh parsley
$^1/_8$ teaspoon salt
$^1/_8$ teaspoon black pepper
Dash of cayenne pepper
Dash of garlic powder
4 (1-pound) pork tenderloins
4 slices bacon

Place the dried apricots in a small bowl and add the boiling water. Let stand for 20 minutes; drain. Melt the butter in a large skillet. Add the green onions, mushrooms and bell pepper. Sauté until tender. Remove from the heat. Add the cooked rice, drained apricots, pecans, parsley, salt, black pepper, cayenne pepper and garlic powder. Stir to mix well. Place the tenderloins on a work surface. Cut a lengthwise slit on top of each tenderloin, being careful not to cut all the way through. Fill 2 tenderloins with the stuffing. Top with the remaining 2 tenderloins, placing the cut side down over the stuffing. Tie with kitchen string to secure. Place the 2 stuffed tenderloins on a rack in a roasting pan and top each with 2 slices bacon. Tent with foil. Bake at 350 degrees for $1^1/_2$ to 2 hours or until a meat thermometer inserted into the thickest porton registers 170 degrees, removing the foil 30 to 40 minutes before done. Let stand for 5 minutes. Remove the string and slice the tenderloins. Garnish with canned apricot halves and parsley sprigs.

Yield: 16 servings

Grilled Pork Tenderloin

$^1/_2$ cup teriyaki sauce
$^1/_2$ cup soy sauce
3 tablespoons brown sugar
2 green onions, chopped
1 garlic clove, minced
1 tablespoon sesame seeds
$^1/_2$ teaspoon ginger
$^1/_2$ teaspoon pepper
1 tablespoon vegetable oil
2 (1-pound) pork tenderloins

Combine the teriyaki sauce, soy sauce, brown sugar, green onions, garlic, sesame seeds, ginger, pepper and oil in a sealable plastic bag. Add the tenderloins and seal the bag tightly. Marinate in the refrigerator for 2 to 4 hours. Remove the tenderloins and discard the marinade. Grill over hot coals for 10 minutes per side or until cooked through.

Yield: 8 servings

Worship the Lord your God, and
his blessing will be on your food and water.
Exodus 23:25

Baked Lemon Veal Scaloppine

1 pound veal scaloppine
$1^1/_2$ cups milk
1 or 2 eggs
$^3/_4$ cup plain or seasoned bread crumbs
2 tablespoons butter
2 tablespoons olive oil
2 tablespoons butter
Juice of $^1/_2$ lemon
Garlic salt to taste
Chopped fresh parsley to taste

Pound the veal on a work surface until thin. Place in a shallow dish and cover with the milk. Let soak in the refrigerator for 1 to 2 hours; drain. Beat the egg in a shallow dish. Dip the veal in the egg and then coat with the bread crumbs. Melt 2 tablespoons butter with the olive oil in a large skillet. Add the veal and brown on both sides. Melt 2 tablespoons butter in a 9×13-inch baking pan in the oven. Tilt to coat the pan evenly with the melted butter. Arrange the browned veal in the pan. Sprinkle with the lemon juice. Season with garlic salt and chopped parsley. Cover with foil. Bake at 325 degrees for 20 to 30 minutes or until cooked through.

Yield: 4 servings

Asparagus Chicken

4 chicken breasts
4 cups water
1/2 teaspoon salt
1 small onion, chopped
1 rib celery, chopped
1/4 cup (1/2 stick) butter
6 tablespoons flour
3 cups chicken broth
1 cup (4 ounces) shredded sharp Cheddar cheese
1 1/2 pounds fresh asparagus, trimmed
1/2 cup buttered bread crumbs

Combine the chicken, water, salt, onion and celery in a saucepan. Simmer for 30 minutes or until the chicken is cooked through. Remove the chicken to a plate to cool. Discard the cooking liquid. Melt the butter in a saucepan. Stir in the flour. Cook until bubbly, stirring constantly. Stir in the chicken broth gradually. Cook until thick, stirring constantly. Add the cheese and cook until the cheese melts, stirring constantly. Remove from the heat. Arrange the asparagus spears in a buttered shallow baking dish. Place the chicken on the asparagus. Cover with the cheese sauce. Sprinkle with the bread crumbs. Bake at 425 degrees for 15 to 20 minutes.

Yield: 4 servings

Oven Fried Parmesan Chicken

1 cup butter cracker crumbs
6 tablespoons grated Parmesan cheese
1 tablespoon dried parsley flakes
$1^1/_2$ teaspoons salt
Dash of garlic powder
$^1/_2$ cup (1 stick) butter, melted
4 to 6 boneless skinless chicken breasts, rinsed and patted dry

Mix the cracker crumbs, cheese, parsley, salt and garlic powder in a shallow dish. Pour the melted butter into a separate shallow dish. Dip the chicken in the melted butter and then coat in the crumb mixture. Arrange in a 9×13-inch baking dish coated with nonstick cooking spray. Bake at 350 degrees for 1 hour or until cooked through.

Yield: 4 to 6 servings

He has shown kindness by giving you rain from heaven and crops in their seasons; he provides you with plenty of food and fills your hearts with joy.
Acts 14:17

Pesto Chicken

6 boneless skinless chicken breasts
1/4 teaspoon salt
1/4 teaspoon pepper
3 ounces cream cheese, softened
1/4 cup prepared pesto
1/2 cup finely chopped green bell pepper
3/4 cup crushed cornflakes
1/2 teaspoon paprika (optional)

Pound the chicken breasts to 1/4 inch thick on a work surface. Sprinkle with the salt and pepper. Combine the cream cheese, pesto and bell pepper in a bowl. Stir to mix well. Spread 2 tablespoons of the cream cheese mixture on each chicken breast. Roll up lengthwise and secure with wooden picks. Combine the cornflake crumbs and paprika in a shallow dish. Coat the rolled chicken in the crumb mixture. Arrange in a 7×11-inch baking dish coated with nonstick cooking spray. Cover and chill for 8 hours. Remove the chicken from the refrigerator 30 minutes before baking. Bake, uncovered, at 350 degrees for 35 minutes or until cooked through. Let stand for 10 minutes before serving.

Yield: 6 servings

Chicken Enchilada Casserole

5 flour tortillas, torn into pieces
4 to 5 tablespoons warm chicken broth
6 chicken breasts, cooked, boned and cubed
1 (14-ounce) can diced tomatoes with green chiles
1 (4-ounce) can chopped green chiles, drained
1 small onion, chopped
2 teaspoons chili powder
1 teaspoon garlic powder
Salt to taste
1 (10-ounce) can cream of chicken soup
1 cup sour cream
1/2 cup mayonnaise
2 tablespoons chicken broth
2 cups (8 ounces) shredded Monterey Jack cheese

Spread the tortilla pieces in the bottom of a 9×13-inch baking dish coated with nonstick cooking spray. Sprinkle with 4 to 5 tablespoons chicken broth. Top with the chicken and spoon the tomatoes with green chiles evenly over the chicken. Sprinkle with the chopped green chiles and top with the onion. Sprinkle with the chili powder and garlic powder and season with salt. Mix the soup, sour cream, mayonnaise and 2 tablespoons chicken broth in a bowl. Pour over the layers. Top with the cheese and cover with foil. Bake at 350 degrees for 50 to 55 minutes. Remove the foil. Reduce the temperature to 275 degrees and bake for 20 to 25 minutes or until the cheese begins to brown.

Yield: 12 servings

Chicken Fettuccini Casserole

1/4 cup (1/2 stick) butter or margarine
1/4 cup flour
1 cup milk
1 cup chicken broth
1 large chicken, cooked, boned and cut into bite-size pieces
5 ounces fettuccini, cooked al dente and drained
2 cups sour cream
1 (10-ounce) package frozen chopped spinach, cooked and well drained
1 (6-ounce) jar sliced mushrooms, drained
1 (8-ounce) can sliced water chestnuts, drained
1 (2-ounce) jar chopped pimento, drained
1/2 cup chopped onion
1/2 cup chopped celery
1/3 cup lemon juice
2 teaspoons seasoned salt
1 teaspoon paprika
1 teaspoon pepper
1 1/2 cups (6 ounces) shredded Monterey Jack cheese

Melt the butter in a saucepan. Add the flour and cook until bubbly, stirring constantly. Stir in the milk and chicken broth gradually. Cook until thick, stirring constantly. Pour into a large bowl. Add the chicken, pasta, sour cream, spinach, mushrooms, water chestnuts, pimento, onion, celery, lemon juice, seasoned salt, paprika and pepper. Stir to mix well. Spoon into a baking dish and top with the cheese. Bake at 350 degrees for 35 to 45 minutes.

Yield: 12 servings

Hot Chicken Salad

2 cups chopped cooked chicken
2 cups chopped celery
$^{1}/_{2}$ cup slivered blanched almonds
$^{1}/_{2}$ teaspoon salt
$^{1}/_{2}$ onion, grated
2 tablespoons lemon juice
1 cup mayonnaise
$^{1}/_{2}$ cup (2 ounces) shredded Cheddar cheese
$^{2}/_{3}$ cup crushed potato chips

Combine the chicken, celery, almonds, salt, onion, lemon juice and mayonnaise in a bowl. Stir to mix well. Spread in a greased shallow baking dish. Mix the cheese and crushed potato chips in a bowl. Sprinkle over the chicken mixture. Bake at 375 degrees for 20 minutes.

Yield: 4 servings

Nehemiah said, "Go and enjoy choice food and sweet drinks, and send some to those who have nothing prepared. This day is sacred to our Lord. Do not grieve for the joy of the Lord is your strength."
Nehemiah 8:10

Lemon Poppy Seed Chicken Casserole

4 chicken breast halves, cooked, boned and shredded
1 cup sour cream
1 (10-ounce) can cream of chicken soup
4 1/2 teaspoons lemon juice
1 tablespoon poppy seeds
35 butter crackers, crushed
1/4 cup (1/2 stick) butter, melted

Place the shredded chicken in a 9-inch square baking dish. Mix the sour cream, soup and lemon juice in a bowl. Pour over the chicken. Mix the poppy seeds and cracker crumbs in a bowl. Sprinkle on top of the casserole. Drizzle with the melted butter. Bake at 350 degrees for 20 to 30 minutes or until the mixture is heated through and the top is golden brown.

Yield: 4 servings

These all look to you to give them their food at the proper time.
Psalm 104:27

Grilled Hawaiian Chicken Breasts

$^1/_2$ cup pineapple juice
1 cup soy sauce
$^1/_2$ cup vinegar
1 cup packed brown sugar
1 teaspoon garlic powder (optional)
6 to 8 boneless skinless chicken breasts, rinsed and patted dry
Pineapple slices

Combine the pineapple juice, soy sauce, vinegar, brown sugar and garlic powder in a saucepan. Simmer until the mixture begins to boil, stirring frequently. Remove from the heat and let cool. Place the chicken in a shallow dish. Pour the marinade over the chicken. Marinate in the refrigerator for at least 30 minutes. Remove the chicken and discard the marinade. Grill over hot coals until cooked through. Grill the pineapple slices and serve on top of the chicken.

Yield: 6 to 8 servings

They were all encouraged and ate some food themselves.
Acts 27:36

"Chic" Chicken

1 tablespoon olive oil
4 ounces fresh mushrooms, halved
1 tablespoon olive oil
4 large boneless skinless chicken breasts, rinsed and patted dry
1 tablespoon Italian herb seasoning
1/2 teaspoon salt
1 teaspoon chicken bouillon granules
1 teaspoon cornstarch
3/4 cup water
1 (14-ounce) can artichoke hearts, drained and quartered
Freshly grated Parmesan cheese to taste

Heat 1 tablespoon olive oil in a medium skillet. Add the mushrooms and sauté for 5 to 8 minutes or until tender. Remove to a bowl. Heat 1 tablespoon olive oil in the same skillet. Sprinkle the chicken with the herb seasoning and salt. Add to the skillet. Cook for 8 to 10 minutes or until the juices run clear when pierced with a fork, turning once during cooking. Remove the chicken to 4 individual plates and keep warm. Mix the bouillon, cornstarch and water in a bowl until smooth. Add to the skillet. Cook over high heat until thickened, stirring constantly. Add the artichoke hearts and cooked mushrooms. Cook until heated through, stirring constantly. Spoon over the chicken and sprinkle with Parmesan cheese.

Yield: 4 servings

Cornish Hens with Wild Rice

2 tablespoons butter or margarine, melted
1/2 cup cashews
1/2 cup sliced green onions
4 (1- to 1 1/4-pound) Cornish game hens
1/4 teaspoon paprika
3/4 cup apricot preserves
2 teaspoons grated orange zest
2 tablespoons orange juice
1 (6-ounce) package long grain and wild rice mix
2 1/3 cups chicken broth

Melt the butter in a skillet. Add the cashews. Sauté over medium-high heat until the cashews are light brown. Remove the cashews to a bowl with a slotted spoon. Add the green onions to the skillet. Sauté until tender. Add to the cashews and set aside.

Rinse the hens inside and out and pat dry. Secure the cavities closed with wooden picks. Tuck the wings under the backs and tie the legs together with string. Sprinkle with the paprika. Place the hens breast side up on a greased rack in a roasting pan. Bake at 350 degrees for 45 minutes. Mix the apricot preserves, orange zest and orange juice in a bowl. Brush 1/3 of this mixture on the hens. Bake the hens for 30 to 45 minutes longer or until the juices run clear when the thigh is pierced with a fork, basting occasionally with the apricot mixture. Keep warm.

Combine the rice mix, contents of the seasoning packet and chicken broth in a saucepan. Bring to a boil and reduce the heat. Simmer, covered, for 25 minutes or until the rice is tender and all the liquid is absorbed. Stir in the cashews and green onions. Place the rice mixture on a serving platter. Arrange the hens on top and brush with the remaining apricot mixture. Garnish with dried apricots, if desired.

Yield: 4 servings

Shrimp Creole

2 tablespoons butter
1 cup chopped onion
1 1/2 cups chopped green bell pepper
1 1/2 cups chopped celery
1 garlic clove, chopped
1/4 cup chopped fresh parsley
4 (8-ounce) cans tomato sauce
1 tablespoon lemon juice
1 tablespoon sugar
1 teaspoon salt
1/2 teaspoon black pepper
1/2 teaspoon cayenne pepper
1/2 teaspoon thyme
1 bay leaf
1 1/2 to 2 pounds deveined peeled shrimp
1/2 teaspoon filé powder
6 cups hot cooked white rice

Melt the butter in a large saucepan. Add the onion, bell pepper, celery, garlic and parsley. Sauté until the vegetables are barely tender. Stir in the tomato sauce, lemon juice, sugar, salt, black pepper, cayenne pepper, thyme and bay leaf. Bring to a boil and add the shrimp. Cook until the shrimp turn pink, stirring frequently. Stir in the filé powder. Remove the bay leaf. Serve the shrimp over the rice.

Yield: 8 servings

Carolina Crab Cakes

$1/4$ cup soft bread crumbs
2 tablespoons milk
1 egg
1 pound backfin crab meat, rinsed and flaked
2 tablespoons Old Bay seasoning
2 tablespoons mayonnaise
1 tablespoon Worcestershire sauce
Salt to taste
Vegetable oil for frying

Combine the bread crumbs, milk and egg in a bowl. Stir to mix well. Add the crab meat, Old Bay seasoning, mayonnaise and Worcestershire sauce. Season with salt. Stir to mix well. Form into small patties. Fry in hot oil in a skillet until brown on both sides. Remove to paper towels to drain. Serve hot with your favorite seafood sauce.

Yield: 2 to 3 servings

Jesus said to them, "Come and have breakfast."
None of the disciples dared ask him, "Who are you?"
They knew it was the Lord.
John 21:12

Crab Mornay

$1/2$ cup (1 stick) butter
6 green onions, chopped
$1/2$ cup chopped fresh parsley
$1/4$ cup chopped bell pepper
2 tablespoons flour
2 cups half-and-half, warmed
Salt to taste
Cayenne pepper to taste
8 ounces baby Swiss cheese, shredded
1 pound crab meat, flaked
8 frozen puff pastry shells, baked according to the package directions

Melt the butter in a skillet. Add the green onions, parsley and bell pepper. Sauté until the vegetables are tender. Stir in the flour. Cook until bubbly, stirring constantly. Stir in the half-and-half gradually. Cook until thickened, stirring constantly. Season with salt and cayenne pepper. Add the cheese and cook until melted, stirring often. Fold in the crab meat. Spoon into the baked pastry shells and garnish with parsley sprigs.

Yield: 8 servings

Grilled Citrus Salmon

$4^1/_2$ teaspoons fresh lemon juice
2 tablespoons olive oil
1 tablespoon butter or margarine
1 tablespoon Dijon mustard
4 garlic cloves, minced
2 teaspoons capers
1 teaspoon basil
1 teaspoon dill weed
2 dashes of salt
2 dashes of cayenne pepper
3 pounds salmon fillets

Combine the lemon juice, olive oil, butter, Dijon mustard, garlic, capers, basil, dill weed, salt and cayenne pepper in a small saucepan. Bring to a boil over medium heat, stirring constantly. Reduce the heat and simmer for 5 minutes. Place the salmon skin side down on a sheet of heavy-duty foil. Fold up the edges to form a pan. Pour the sauce over the salmon. Place over medium-hot coals on a grill with a lid. Cook with the lid down for 10 to 12 minutes or until the fish flakes easily.

Yield: 8 servings

Savory Summer Pie

1 (1-crust) refrigerator pie pastry
2 tablespoons olive oil
1 small red bell pepper, chopped
1/2 purple onion, chopped
2 garlic cloves, minced
2 tablespoons chopped fresh basil
4 eggs
1 cup half-and-half
1 teaspoon salt
1/2 teaspoon pepper
2 cups (8 ounces) shredded Monterey Jack cheese
1/3 cup grated Parmesan cheese
3 plum tomatoes, cut into 1/4-inch slices

Fit the pastry into a 9-inch deep-dish tart pan. Prick the bottom and side with a fork. Bake at 425 degrees for 10 minutes. Remove to a wire rack to cool.

Heat the olive oil in a skillet. Add the bell pepper, onion and garlic. Sauté for 5 minutes or until tender. Stir in the basil and remove from the heat. Whisk the eggs, half-and-half, salt and pepper in a bowl. Stir in the sautéed vegetables, Monterey Jack cheese and Parmesan cheese. Pour into the baked crust and arrange the tomato slices on top. Bake at 375 degrees for 45 to 50 minutes or until set, covering the edges with foil after 30 minutes of baking to prevent excess browning. Remove to a wire rack and let cool for 5 minutes before cutting.

Yield: 6 to 8 servings

Vegetarian Green Enchiladas

1 (10-ounce) package frozen chopped spinach, thawed and drained
1 cup sour cream
1 (10-ounce) can cream of chicken soup
1 (4-ounce) can green chiles, chopped and drained
2 tablespoons chopped green onions
2 cups vegetable oil, or 1 (14-ounce) can chicken broth, warmed
12 corn tortillas
3/4 cup finely chopped onion
4 cups (16 ounces) shredded Monterey Jack cheese

Place the spinach, sour cream, soup, green chiles and green onions in a blender. Process until smooth. Pour the warmed oil into a shallow bowl. Dip 1 tortilla in the oil to coat and place on a work surface. Place 1 tablespoon of the chopped green onions and 1 tablespoon cheese at 1 end of the tortilla. Roll up and place seam side down in a greased baking dish. Repeat with the remaining tortillas, green onions and cheese, arranging in a single layer in the baking dish. Pour the spinach mixture over the tortillas and sprinkle with the remaining cheese. Bake at 325 degrees for 30 minutes.

Yield: 6 servings

Roasted Vegetable Lasagna

1 pound plum tomatoes, cut into 1/4-inch slices
1 pound zucchini, cut into 1/4-inch slices
1 pound yellow squash, cut into 1/4-inch slices
8 ounces mushroom caps, cut into 1/4-inch slices
2 green bell peppers, cut into strips (optional)
2 red bell peppers, cut into strips (optional)
1 teaspoon salt
1 tablespoon olive oil
3 (14-ounce) cans diced tomatoes with garlic
12 oven-ready lasagna noodles
1 egg white
2 (15-ounce) containers light ricotta cheese
2 tablespoons prepared pesto
1/3 cup freshly grated Parmesan cheese
2 cups (8 ounces) shredded low-fat mozzarella cheese

Combine the tomatoes, zucchini, yellow squash, mushrooms, green bell peppers, red bell peppers, salt and olive oil in a large bowl. Toss to coat. Arrange on a baking sheet coated with nonstick cooking spray. Bake at 475 degrees for 30 minutes. Remove to a wire rack to cool.

Spread 1 can of the diced tomatoes in a 9×13-inch baking pan coated with nonstick cooking spray. Top with 3 lasagna noodles. Mix the egg white, ricotta cheese, pesto and Parmesan cheese in a bowl. Spread 1 1/4 cups over the noodles in the baking dish. Top with 1/3 of the roasted vegetables. Sprinkle with 1/2 cup of the mozzarella cheese. Repeat the layers. Add the final can of tomatoes, 3 noodles, remaining ricotta cheese mixture and remaining vegetables. Top with the final 3 noodles and 1 cup mozzarella cheese. Cover with foil. Bake at 375 degrees for 30 minutes.

Yield: 12 servings

And now abideth faith, hope, love;
but the greatest of these is love.

I Corinthians 13:13

For twenty-seven years, Helen Kraatz presided as the official Church Hostess. During her tenure, she helped plan over 1,800 weddings. One could always count on seeing Helen and her team of ladies on Wednesday night as they served supper in the Fellowship Hall. As in any family, the stories of the people, places, and events of the church are endless. Whether it was High School Bible fellowships, GA coronations, Father-Daughter Dinners, Sweetheart Banquets, or just friends gathering to share their joys and sorrows, a table laden with good food was usually a part of such an occasion.

They devoted themselves to the apostles' teachings and to the fellowship, to the breaking of bread and to prayer (Acts 2:24). As members spent time around the tables, they grew to be a true family of faith, hope, and love.

Cakes

Elegant Layered Apple Cake

Cake

3 cups flour
$1^1/_2$ teaspoons baking soda
$^1/_2$ teaspoon salt
3 cups grated peeled tart apples
$^1/_2$ cup chopped walnuts
1 teaspoon grated lemon zest
2 cups sugar
$1^1/_2$ cups vegetable oil
2 eggs

Frosting

8 ounces cream cheese, softened
$^1/_2$ cup (1 stick) butter, softened
1 (1-pound) package confectioners' sugar
1 teaspoon vanilla extract
1 cup finely chopped walnuts

For the cake, mix the flour, baking soda and salt in a bowl. Mix the apples, walnuts and lemon zest in a bowl. Combine the sugar, oil and eggs in a large bowl. Mix well with a wooden spoon. Add the dry ingredients and stir to mix well. Stir in the apple mixture until well combined. Pour into 3 greased and floured 9-inch round cake pans. Bake at 350 degrees for 30 to 40 minutes or until the cake springs back when pressed lightly. Cool in the pans for 10 minutes. Remove to a wire rack to cool completely.

For the frosting, beat the cream cheese and butter in a mixing bowl until light and fluffy. Beat in the confectioners' sugar gradually. Add the vanilla and beat until smooth. Spread the frosting between the layers and over the top and side of the cooled cake. Press the chopped walnuts into the side of the cake. Chill until ready to serve.

Yield: 12 servings

Note: Make $1^1/_2$ times the frosting recipe if you prefer a generously frosted cake.

Apricot Nectar Cake

1 (18-ounce) box yellow cake mix
1 (3-ounce) package lemon gelatin
3/4 cup apricot nectar
3/4 cup vegetable oil
4 eggs, beaten
2 teaspoons lemon extract
1 cup confectioners' sugar
Juice of 1 lemon

Combine the cake mix, gelatin, apricot nectar, oil, eggs and lemon extract in a large bowl. Beat with an electric mixer until smooth. Pour into a greased and floured bundt pan. Bake at 325 degrees for 1 hour or until a wooden pick inserted in the center comes out clean. Cool in the pan for 10 minutes. Invert onto a serving plate. Mix the confectioners' sugar and lemon juice in a small bowl. Drizzle over the hot cake. Let cool before slicing.

Yield: 16 servings

The eyes of all look to you and
you give them their food at the proper time.
Psalm 145:15

Blackberry Jam Cake

2 cups blackberry jam
2 cups flour
1 cup (2 sticks) butter, softened
2 cups sugar
1 cup milk
5 egg yolks, well beaten
1 teaspoon cinnamon
1/2 teaspoon cloves
1 teaspoon allspice
1 teaspoon nutmeg
1 cup flour
1 teaspoon baking soda
1 tablespoon hot water
5 egg whites
Caramel Icing (page 143)

Mix the jam and 2 cups flour in a bowl. Cream the butter and sugar in a large mixing bowl until light and fluffy. Stir in the jam mixture. Add the milk and egg yolks and stir to mix well. Combine the cinnamon, cloves, allspice, nutmeg and 1 cup flour in a bowl. Dissolve the baking soda in the hot water in a small bowl. Stir into the spice mixture. Add to the jam mixture. Stir to mix well. Beat the egg whites in a bowl until stiff peaks form. Fold into the batter. Pour into 3 greased and floured 9-inch round cake pans. Bake at 350 degrees for 30 minutes or until a wooden pick inserted in the center comes out clean. Cool in the pans for 10 minutes. Remove to a wire rack to cool completely. Spread the Caramel Icing between the layers and over the top and side of the cooled cake.

Yield: 12 servings

Caramel Icing

1/2 cup sugar
3/4 cup evaporated milk
1/4 cup water
2 cups sugar
1/2 cup (1 stick) butter
1 cup chopped nuts

Cook 1/2 cup sugar in a skillet until brown. Combine the evaporated milk, water, 2 cups sugar and butter in a heavy saucepan. Bring to a boil. Stir in the browned sugar. Cook to 234 to 240 degrees on a candy thermometer, soft-ball stage. Remove from the heat and beat to spreading consistency. Stir in the nuts or press the nuts onto the cake after icing.

Yield: 3 cups

A generous man will himself be blessed, for he shares his food with the poor.
Proverbs 22:9

Carrot Cake with Cream Cheese Frosting

Cake

3 cups grated carrots
2 cups flour
2 cups sugar
2 teaspoons baking soda
1 teaspoon baking powder
1/2 teaspoon salt
1 teaspoon cinnamon
4 eggs, well beaten
1 1/4 cups vegetable oil
1 teaspoon vanilla extract

Frosting

12 ounces cream cheese, softened
3/4 cup (1 1/2 sticks) butter, softened
5 to 6 cups confectioners' sugar
1 1/2 teaspoons vanilla extract
1 cup pecans, chopped

For the cake, mix the carrots, flour, sugar, baking soda, baking powder, salt and cinnamon in a bowl. Stir in the eggs, oil and vanilla. Pour into 3 greased and floured 9-inch round cake pans. Bake at 350 degrees for 30 minutes or until a wooden pick inserted in the center comes out clean. Cool in the pans for 10 minutes. Remove to a wire rack to cool completely.

For the frosting, beat the cream cheese and butter in a mixing bowl until light and fluffy. Beat in the confectioners' sugar gradually. Add the vanilla and beat until smooth. Spread the frosting between the layers and over the top and side of the cooled cake. Sprinkle the chopped pecans on top.

Yield: 12 servings

Lemon Raspberry Cake

Cake

1 cup shortening
2 cups sugar
4 eggs
3 cups sifted cake flour
2 1/2 teaspoons baking powder
1/2 teaspoon salt
1 cup milk
1 teaspoon each vanilla extract and almond extract
1 (10-ounce) jar seedless raspberry preserves

Frosting

1 1/4 cups (2 1/2 sticks) butter or margarine, softened
2 teaspoons grated lemon zest
1 tablespoon lemon juice
3 cups sifted confectioners' sugar

For the cake, beat the shortening in a large bowl at medium speed with an electric mixer until creamy. Add the sugar gradually. Beat in the eggs 1 at a time. Combine the flour, baking powder and salt in a bowl. Add to the egg mixture alternately with the milk, beginning and ending with the dry ingredients and beating well after each addition. Stir in the vanilla and almond extract. Pour into 3 greased and floured 9-inch round cake pans. Bake at 375 degrees for 18 to 20 minutes or until a wooden pick inserted in the center comes out clean. Cool in the pans for 10 minutes. Remove to a wire rack to cool completely. Slice the cooled layers into halves horizontally to make 6 layers. Place 1 layer cut side up on a serving plate. Spread with 3 tablespoons of the raspberry preserves. Repeat with the remaining 5 layers, placing the top layer cut side down and omitting the preserves on the top layer.

For the frosting, beat the butter, lemon zest and lemon juice in a bowl with an electric mixer until creamy. Beat in the confectioners' sugar gradually and beat until smooth. Spread 1 3/4 cups of the frosting between the layers and over the top and side of the cooled cake. Pipe the remaining frosting on top of the cake using a star tip. Garnish with lemon slices. Chill in an airtight container until ready to serve.

Yield: 12 servings

Lemon Poppy Seed Cake

1 (18-ounce) box yellow cake mix
1/2 cup sugar
1/3 cup vegetable oil
1/4 cup water
1 cup plain yogurt
3 eggs, or 1 cup egg substitute
3 tablespoons lemon juice
2 tablespoons poppy seeds
1/2 cup sifted confectioners' sugar
2 tablespoons lemon juice

Mix the cake mix and sugar in a large bowl. Add the oil, water, yogurt, eggs and 3 tablespoons lemon juice. Beat at medium speed with an electric mixer for 6 minutes. Stir in the poppy seeds. Pour into a greased and floured bundt pan. Bake at 350 degrees for 40 minutes or until a wooden pick inserted in the center comes out clean. Cool in the pan for 10 minutes. Remove to a wire rack to cool completely. Stir the confectioners' sugar and 2 tablespoons lemon juice in a bowl until smooth. Drizzle over the cooled cake on a serving plate.

Yield: 16 servings

Strawberry Cake

1 (18-ounce) box white cake mix
4 eggs
1 cup vegetable oil
1/2 cup water
3 tablespoons flour
1 (3-ounce) package strawberry gelatin
1 (10-ounce) package frozen sweetened strawberries, thawed
1/2 cup (1 stick) butter, softened
1 (1-pound) package confectioners' sugar

Combine the cake mix, eggs, oil, water, flour and gelatin in a large bowl. Stir to mix well. Stir in half the package of strawberries and juice. Pour into a greased and floured 9×13-inch cake pan. Bake at 350 degrees for 35 to 40 minutes or until a wooden pick inserted in the center comes out clean. Remove to a wire rack to cool. Beat the butter and remaining half of the strawberries and juice in a bowl. Beat in the confectioners' sugar gradually until blended. Frost the cooled cake with the icing.

Yield: 15 servings

Coffee Royal Cake

1 (18-ounce) box yellow cake mix
1 (18-ounce) box chocolate cake mix
$1\frac{1}{2}$ cups whipping cream
3 tablespoons instant coffee powder
$\frac{1}{3}$ cup sugar
1 (11-ounce) jar raspberry preserves
1 cup whipping cream
Shaved chocolate

Prepare the yellow cake mix and chocolate cake mix according to the package directions. Bake each cake in 2 greased and floured 9-inch round cake pans. Let cool. Split 1 yellow layer and 1 chocolate layer crosswise. Freeze remaining layers for future use.

Combine $1\frac{1}{2}$ cups whipping cream, the instant coffee and sugar in a bowl. Chill until very cold. Whip until stiff. Place 1 yellow cake layer on a serving plate. Spread with half the raspberry preserves. Spread with $\frac{1}{3}$ of the coffee filling. Top with a chocolate cake layer. Spread with $\frac{1}{3}$ of the coffee filling. Top with a yellow cake layer. Spread with the remaining raspberry preserves. Spread with the remaining coffee filling. Top with a chocolate cake layer. Whip 1 cup whipping cream until stiff. Spread over the top of the cake and sprinkle with shaved chocolate. Chill until ready to serve.

Yield: 16 servings

Coconut Cake

2 (6-ounce) packages frozen unsweetened shredded coconut
2 cups sugar
2 cups sour cream
1 (18-ounce) box butter-recipe cake mix
$3^1/2$ cups frozen whipped topping, thawed
1 (6-ounce) package frozen unsweetened shredded coconut

Mix 2 packages coconut, the sugar and sour cream in a bowl. Cover and chill for 24 hours. Prepare the cake mix according to the package directions. Bake the cake in 2 greased and floured 9-inch round cake pans. Let cool. Slice the cooled layers into halves horizontally to make 4 layers. Spread the coconut mixture between the layers and over the top and side of the cooled cake on a serving plate. Spread the whipped topping over the coconut mixture. Sprinkle with 1 package coconut. Chill in an airtight container for 5 days before serving. May be frozen.

Yield: 12 servings

Chocolate Sheet Cake

Cake

2 cups sugar
2 cups flour
1 teaspoon cinnamon
1/2 cup (1 stick) butter or margarine
1/2 cup shortening
1/4 cup baking cocoa
1 cup water
2 eggs
1/2 cup buttermilk
1 teaspoon baking soda
1 teaspoon vanilla extract

Icing

7 tablespoons evaporated milk or cream
1/4 cup baking cocoa
1/2 cup (1 stick) butter or margarine
1 (1-pound) package confectioners' sugar
1 teaspoon vanilla extract
1 cup chopped nuts (optional)

For the cake, mix the sugar, flour and cinnamon in a large bowl. Combine the butter, shortening, baking cocoa and water in a saucepan. Bring to a boil. Add to the dry ingredients and stir until smooth. Add the eggs 1 at a time, beating well after each addition. Mix the buttermilk and baking soda in a small bowl. Stir into the batter. Add the vanilla and stir to mix well. Pour into a greased and floured 9×13-inch cake pan. Bake at 400 degrees for 30 to 40 minutes or until a wooden pick inserted in the center comes out clean. Remove to a wire rack and let cool slightly.

For the icing, stir the evaporated milk gradually into the baking cocoa in a saucepan. Add the butter. Cook until melted and smooth, stirring constantly. Remove from the heat and add the confectioners' sugar and vanilla. Stir until smooth. Stir in the nuts. Pour over the warm cake. Let cool before cutting.

Yield: 15 servings

Cola Cake

Cake

1 cup (2 sticks) butter
3 tablespoons baking cocoa
$1\frac{1}{2}$ cups cold cola (not diet or decaffeinated)
2 cups flour
2 cups sugar
$\frac{1}{2}$ cup buttermilk
2 eggs, beaten
1 teaspoon baking soda
1 teaspoon vanilla extract
$1\frac{1}{2}$ cups miniature marshmallows

Frosting

$\frac{1}{2}$ cup (1 stick) butter
3 tablespoons baking cocoa
6 tablespoons cold cola (not diet or decaffeinated)
1 (1-pound) package confectioners' sugar
1 cup chopped pecans (optional)

For the cake, combine the butter, baking cocoa and cola in a saucepan. Bring to a boil, whisking constantly. Combine the flour and sugar in a large bowl. Add the hot cola mixture. Beat at low speed with an electric mixer until blended. Add the buttermilk, eggs, baking soda and vanilla. Beat at low to medium speed until well mixed. Stir in the marshmallows. Pour into a greased and floured 10×15-inch cake pan. Bake at 350 degrees for 30 to 35 minutes or until a wooden pick inserted in the center comes out clean. Remove to a wire rack.

For the frosting, combine the butter, baking cocoa and cola in a saucepan. Bring to a boil, whisking constantly. Pour over the confectioners' sugar in a bowl. Stir until smooth. Stir in the pecans. Pour over the hot cake. Let cool before cutting.

Yield: 15 servings

Ebony and Ivory Chocolate Cake

1 (18-ounce) box yellow cake mix
1 (3-ounce) package chocolate instant pudding mix
1/2 cup sugar
3/4 cup water
3/4 cup vegetable oil
4 eggs
1 cup sour cream
1 1/2 cups semisweet chocolate chips
4 ounces white chocolate
2 1/2 tablespoons shortening
1/2 cup semisweet chocolate chips
2 1/2 tablespoons shortening

Stir the cake mix, pudding mix and sugar in a large bowl with a wooden spoon. Add the water and oil. Beat at low speed with an electric mixer until blended. Add the eggs 1 at a time, beating well after each addition. Beat at medium speed for 2 minutes. Add the sour cream and beat at medium speed for 30 seconds. Stir in 2 cups chocolate chips. Pour into a bundt pan generously coated with nonstick cooking spray. Bake at 350 degrees for 1 hour or until a wooden pick inserted in the center comes out clean. Remove to a wire rack and let cool in the pan for 1 hour. Invert onto a serving plate and let cool completely.

Combine the white chocolate and 2 1/2 tablespoons shortening in a small saucepan. Cook over low heat until melted, stirring frequently. Drizzle over the cake. Combine 1/2 cup chocolate chips and 2 1/2 tablespoons shortening in a small saucepan. Cook over low heat until melted, stirring frequently. Drizzle over the white chocolate coating.

Yield: 16 servings

Four-Flavor Cake

1 cup (2 sticks) butter, softened
3 cups sugar
1/2 cup vegetable oil
5 eggs
3 cups flour
1 cup lukewarm milk
1 teaspoon vanilla extract
1 teaspoon almond extract
1 teaspoon lemon extract
1 teaspoon orange extract

Cream the butter, sugar and oil in a mixing bowl until light and fluffy. Add the eggs 1 at a time, beating well after each addition. Add a few tablespoons of the flour and beat well. Add a few tablespoons of the milk and beat well. Add the flour alternately with the milk, ending with the flour and beating well after each addition. Add the vanilla, almond extract, lemon extract and orange extract. Beat to mix well. Pour into a greased and floured 10-inch tube pan. Bake at 325 degrees for 1 to 1 1/4 hours or until a wooden pick inserted in the center comes out clean. Let cool in the pan for 4 minutes. Remove to a wire rack and let cool completely.

Yield: 16 servings

Eat honey, my son, for it is good;
honey from the comb is sweet to your taste.
Proverbs 24:13

Honey Bun Cake

1 (18-ounce) box butter-recipe cake mix
4 eggs
3/4 cup vegetable oil
1 cup sour cream
1 cup packed brown sugar
2 tablespoons cinnamon
2 cups confectioners' sugar
6 tablespoons milk
1 teaspoon vanilla extract

Combine the cake mix, eggs, oil and sour cream in a large bowl. Beat until well mixed. Pour half the batter into a greased and floured 9×13-inch cake pan. Mix the brown sugar and cinnamon in a small bowl. Sprinkle over the batter in the pan and swirl with a knife. Top with the remaining batter. Bake at 350 degrees for 30 to 35 minutes. Remove to a wire rack. The cake will fall when removed from the oven. Combine the confectioners' sugar, milk and vanilla in a bowl. Stir until smooth. Spread over the hot cake. Let cool before cutting.

Yield: 15 servings

She is like the merchant ships, bringing her food from afar.
Proverbs 31:14

Italian Cream Cake

Cake

1 cup buttermilk
1 teaspoon baking soda
2 cups sugar
1/2 cup (1 stick) margarine, softened
1/2 cup shortening
5 egg yolks
2 cups sifted flour
1 teaspoon vanilla extract
5 egg whites
1 cup pecans, chopped
1 (7-ounce) can flaked coconut

Frosting

8 ounces cream cheese, softened
1/2 cup (1 stick) butter, softened
1 (1-pound) package confectioners' sugar
1 teaspoon vanilla extract

For the cake, combine the buttermilk and baking soda in a small bowl. Let stand for a few minutes. Cream the sugar, margarine and shortening in a large mixing bowl until light and fluffy. Add the egg yolks 1 at a time, beating well after each addition. Beat in the buttermilk mixture alternately with the flour. Stir in the vanilla. Beat the egg whites in a bowl until stiff peaks form. Fold into the batter. Fold in the pecans and coconut. Pour into 3 greased and floured 9-inch round cake pans. Bake at 325 degrees for 25 minutes or until a wooden pick inserted in the center comes out clean. Cool in the pans for 10 minutes. Remove to a wire rack to cool completely.

For the frosting, beat the cream cheese and butter in a mixing bowl until light and fluffy. Beat in the confectioners' sugar gradually. Add the vanilla and beat until smooth. Spread the frosting between the layers and over the top and side of the cooled cake.

Yield: 12 servings

Mom Penn's Pound Cake

2 cups (4 sticks) butter, softened
$2^1/_2$ cups sugar
9 eggs, at room temperature
4 cups cake flour
1 teaspoon orange extract

Beat the butter in a bowl with an electric mixer until light and fluffy. Beat in the sugar $^1/_2$ cup at a time. Add the eggs 1 at a time, beating well after each addition. Beat in the flour gradually. Add the orange extract. Beat at high speed for 2 to 3 minutes. Pour into a greased and floured tube pan. Bake at 250 degrees for 40 minutes. Increase the temperature to 325 degrees and bake for 40 minutes longer or until a wooden pick inserted in the center comes out clean. Let cool in the pan for 10 minutes. Remove to a wire rack and let cool completely.

Yield: 16 servings

And after taking some food, he regained his strength
Acts 9:19

Praline Cheesecake

1 cup graham cracker crumbs
1/4 cup finely chopped pecans
2 tablespoons sugar
5 1/3 tablespoons butter, melted
24 ounces cream cheese, softened
1 cup packed brown sugar
3 eggs
2 teaspoons vanilla extract

Combine the graham cracker crumbs, chopped pecans, sugar and melted butter in a bowl. Stir to mix well. Press onto the bottom and 1 inch up the side of a 9-inch springform pan. Bake at 350 degrees for 8 minutes. Place on a wire rack.

Beat the cream cheese in a bowl at high speed with an electric mixer until light and fluffy. Add the brown sugar and beat well. Add the eggs 1 at a time, beating well after each addition. Stir in the vanilla. Pour into the prepared crust. Bake at 325 degrees for 40 minutes. Turn off the oven and leave the oven door ajar. Let the cheesecake stand in the oven for 30 minutes. Remove to a wire rack and let cool completely. Cover and chill for at least 8 hours or up to several days. Loosen from the side of the pan with a sharp knife and remove the side. Garnish with whipped cream and toasted pecans.

Yield: 8 servings

Christmas Cheesecake

Crust

2 cups graham cracker crumbs
1/4 cup coarsely ground pecans
5 1/3 tablespoons unsalted butter, melted

Filling and Decoration

40 ounces cream cheese, softened
2 1/4 cups sugar
1 cup sour cream
6 eggs
1/3 cup flour
1 tablespoon each grated orange zest and grated lemon zest
1 teaspoon fresh lemon juice
2 teaspoons vanilla extract
1/2 cup whipping cream
2 tablespoons sugar
2/3 cup raspberry preserves or strawberry preserves
2 kiwifruit, peeled and thinly sliced

For the crust, combine all the ingredients in a bowl. Stir to mix well. Press onto the bottom and up the side of a greased 10-inch springform pan. Freeze until firm.

For the filling, beat the cream cheese, 2 1/4 cups sugar and sour cream in a large bowl at medium-high speed with an electric mixer for 5 minutes. Add the eggs 1 at a time, beating well after each addition. Beat in the flour, orange zest, lemon zest, lemon juice and vanilla. Pour into the frozen crust. Bake at 350 degrees for 1 to 1 1/4 hours or until the top is light brown and the center is not quite set. Remove to a wire rack and let cool for 2 hours. Cover and chill for 8 hours. Loosen from the side of the pan with a sharp knife and remove the side.

For the decoration, beat the whipping cream in a chilled bowl at medium-high speed with an electric mixer until soft peaks form. Sprinkle with 2 tablespoons sugar and beat until stiff peaks form. Place in a pastry bag fitted with a tip. Pipe a border around the top edge of the cheesecake. Spread the preserves on top of the cake to the edge of the border. Arrange the sliced kiwifruit in spirals near the border.

Yield: 10 servings

Peppermint Chocolate Cheesecake

2 cups chocolate sandwich cookie crumbs
5 1/3 tablespoons unsalted butter, melted
48 ounces cream cheese, softened
2 cups sugar
6 eggs
1/2 cup flour
1 cup sour cream
2 teaspoons vanilla extract
1/2 teaspoon peppermint extract
1 cup semisweet chocolate chips, melted and cooled
1 (12-ounce) package semisweet chocolate chunks
1 cup crushed candy canes
2 tablespoons flour
Whipped cream
1/4 cup crushed candy canes

Combine the cookie crumbs, and melted butter in a bowl. Stir to mix well. Press onto the bottom and up the side of a greased 10-inch springform pan. Freeze until firm.

Beat the cream cheese and sugar in a large bowl at medium-high speed with an electric mixer for 5 minutes. Add the eggs 1 at a time, beating well after each addition. Beat in 1/2 cup flour, the sour cream, vanilla, peppermint extract and melted chocolate. Combine the chocolate chunks, 1 cup crushed candy canes and 2 tablespoons flour in a bowl. Toss to coat. Fold into the batter. Pour into the frozen crust. Bake at 350 degrees for 1 to 1 1/4 hours or until the top is light brown. Remove to a wire rack and let cool for 2 hours. Cover and chill for 8 hours. Loosen from the side of the pan with a sharp knife and remove the side. Spread whipped cream over the top of the cheesecake and sprinkle with 1/4 cup crushed candy canes.

Yield: 10 servings

Even so, come, Lord Jesus. The grace of our Lord Jesus Christ be with you all.

Revelation 22:20-21

Just as Doris Sparks and Betty Hallman in years past could always be counted upon to bring delicious food for whatever the occasion, dinners are still delivered to the sick or bereaved. Homes are still opened for youth events, babies are still held and loved in the church nursery, the Clothes Closet still provides clothing for those in need, and women still serve the community in multitudes of ways. Yes, women are still reaching out to a hungry world and sharing God's love with every deed.

A legacy of hospitality and service began with the formation of Park Cities Baptist Church and continues to this day. May our faith add to the heritage of a great church and become a gift to those who follow us. May we continue to open our homes and our hearts to others, and may the grace of our Lord Jesus Christ be with you all as you serve those around you

For Such a Time as This.

Desserts and Cookies

Favorite Apple Pie

$1^1/_4$ cups sugar
$^1/_8$ teaspoon salt
1 small lemon, sliced and seeded
$^1/_4$ cup water
3 pounds tart apples, peeled, cored and cut into eighths
1 tablespoon flour
$^1/_2$ teaspoon cinnamon
1 tablespoon butter
1 (2-crust) pie pastry, chilled
1 egg yolk
1 tablespoon milk

Combine the sugar, salt, lemon slices and water in a large skillet. Cook, covered, over medium heat until the sugar begins to dissolve. Add the apples a few at a time in a single layer. Simmer, uncovered, for 5 to 7 minutes or until slightly tender. Remove the apples with a slotted spoon to waxed paper. Remove and discard the lemon slices. Mix the flour and cinnamon in a small bowl. Add to the syrup. Cook until reduced to $^1/_2$ cup, stirring constantly. Stir in the butter. Remove from the heat and let cool. Fit 1 pie pastry into a 9-inch pie plate. Spoon the apples and syrup into the pie shell. Cut the remaining pastry into strips. Arrange lattice-fashion over the pie. Mix the egg yolk and milk in a small bowl. Brush over the piecrust. Bake at 400 degrees for 45 minutes. Cool on a wire rack.

Yield: 8 servings

Buttermilk Pie

$^{1}/_{2}$ cup (1 stick) butter, softened
2 cups sugar
3 eggs, beaten
3 tablespoons flour
1 cup buttermilk
1 teaspoon vanilla extract
Dash of nutmeg
1 unbaked (9-inch) pie shell

Cream the butter and sugar in a mixing bowl until light and fluffy. Beat in the eggs and flour. Add the buttermilk, vanilla and nutmeg and beat to mix well. Pour into the pie shell. Bake at 350 degrees for 45 minutes or until set. Cool on a wire rack.

Yield: 8 servings

Chocolate Pecan Pie

1 cup sugar
$^{1}/_{2}$ cup flour
2 eggs, beaten
$^{1}/_{2}$ cup (1 stick) butter, melted and cooled
1 cup chocolate chips
$^{1}/_{2}$ cup pecan pieces
1 teaspoon vanilla extract
1 unbaked (9-inch) pie shell

Mix the sugar and flour in a bowl. Add the eggs and melted butter and stir to mix well. Stir in the chocolate chips, pecans and vanilla. Pour into the pie shell. Bake at 350 degrees for 30 minutes or until set. Cool on a wire rack.

Yield: 8 servings

Special Coconut Pie

1 1/2 cups milk
1/2 cup evaporated milk
3/4 cup sugar
1/4 cup flour
3 egg yolks, beaten
2 tablespoons margarine
1 teaspoon vanilla extract
1 cup flaked coconut
1 baked (10-inch) pie shell
Whipped cream
Flaked coconut

Combine the milk, evaporated milk, sugar and flour in a large saucepan. Cook over medium heat until thickened, stirring constantly. Beat in the egg yolks and cook until very thick, stirring constantly. Remove from the heat and add the margarine, vanilla and coconut. Stir until the margarine melts. Pour into the pie shell and let cool. Top with whipped cream and sprinkle with coconut.

Yield: 8 servings

She gets up while it is still dark; she provides
food for her family and portions for her servant girls.
Proverbs 31:15

Fudge Pie

1 cup (2 sticks) margarine
4 ounces unsweetened chocolate
4 eggs, beaten
2 cups sugar
1/2 cup flour
1/2 teaspoon salt
2 teaspoons vanilla extract
2/3 cup pecans, chopped (optional)

Melt the margarine and chocolate in a saucepan over low heat, stirring occasionally. Remove from the heat and let cool. Mix the eggs and sugar in a large bowl. Stir in the cooled chocolate mixture. Add the flour, salt, vanilla and pecans and stir to mix well. Pour into a 9-inch square baking dish. Bake at 350 degrees for 30 to 40 minutes. Cool on a wire rack. Cut into squares when cool and serve with ice cream.

Yield: 9 servings

Pecan Pie

1/2 cup (1 stick) butter
1 cup light corn syrup
1 cup sugar
3 eggs, beaten
1 teaspoon vanilla extract
Dash of salt
1 cup pecans, chopped
1 unbaked (9-inch) pie shell

Cook the butter in a saucepan until golden brown; do not allow to burn. Remove from the heat and allow to cool. Mix the corn syrup, sugar, eggs, vanilla and salt in a bowl. Stir in the browned butter and pecans. Pour into the pie shell. Bake at 325 degrees for 50 minutes. Cool on a wire rack.

Yield: 8 servings

Sweet Potato Pie

2½ cups mashed cooked sweet potatoes (about 3 medium)
½ cup (1 stick) butter, softened
2 cups sugar
1 (14-ounce) can evaporated milk
4 eggs, beaten
1 teaspoon cinnamon
½ teaspoon salt
½ teaspoon nutmeg
¼ teaspoon cloves
1 unbaked (9-inch) pie shell

Beat the sweet potatoes and butter in a bowl until smooth. Add the sugar, evaporated milk, eggs, cinnamon, salt, nutmeg and cloves. Mix until smooth. Pour into the pie shell. Bake at 350 degrees for 1 hour and 10 minutes or until set. Cool on a wire rack.

Yield: 8 servings

Taste and see that the Lord is good.
Psalm 34:8

Heavenly Goo Pie

1 cup graham cracker crumbs
$1/4$ cup ($1/2$ stick) margarine, melted
$1\frac{1}{4}$ cups confectioners' sugar
2 egg yolks
$1/4$ cup ($1/2$ stick) margarine, melted
1 teaspoon vanilla extract
2 egg whites
1 cup whipping cream, whipped
1 cup broken nuts

Mix the graham cracker crumbs and $1/4$ cup melted margarine in a bowl. Press half the crumb mixture into a lightly greased 9×13-inch baking dish. Combine the confectioners' sugar, egg yolks, $1/4$ cup melted margarine and vanilla in a large bowl. Stir to mix well. Beat the egg whites in a bowl until stiff peaks form. Fold into the egg yolk mixture. Fold in the whipped cream and nuts. Pour into the prepared crust. Top with the remaining crumb mixture. Cover with foil and freeze until firm. Serve frozen.

Yield: 15 servings

Do not forget to entertain strangers, for by so doing,
some people have entertained angels without knowing it.
Hebrews 13:2

Kathleen York's Tutti-Frutti Ice Cream

4 cups half-and-half
2 cups heavy cream
3 cups sugar
Juice of 3 oranges
Juice of 3 lemons
3 bananas, mashed

Combine the half-and-half, cream, sugar, orange juice, lemon juice and mashed bananas in a bowl. Stir to mix well. Pour into an ice cream freezer container. Freeze using the manufacturer's directions.

Yield: 2 quarts

Homemade Vanilla Ice Cream

4 cups milk, scalded
2 3/4 cups sugar
3/4 teaspoon salt
4 cups half-and-half
4 cups heavy cream
2 tablespoons vanilla extract

Combine the scalded milk, sugar and salt in a large bowl. Stir until the sugar dissolves. Stir in the half-and-half, cream and vanilla. Cover and chill. Pour into an ice cream freezer container. Freeze using the manufacturer's directions.

Yield: 1 gallon

Chocolate Sauce

2 ounces unsweetened chocolate
6 tablespoons margarine
1 1/2 cups sugar
1/4 teaspoon salt
Pinch of cream of tartar
1 cup evaporated milk
1 teaspoon vanilla extract

Place the chocolate and margarine in the top of a double boiler. Cook over simmering water until melted. Stir in the sugar gradually. Add the salt and cream of tartar. Stir in the evaporated milk gradually. Add the vanilla and stir to mix. Cook, covered, for 30 minutes. Do not overcook. Pour into a bowl and let cool. Cover and chill until ready to serve. Pour over ice cream.

Yield: 3 cups

Then she went on her way and ate something and her face was no longer downcast.
I Samuel 1:18

Mom's Four-Layer Dessert

$^{1}/_{2}$ cup (1 stick) margarine, melted
1 cup flour
1 cup pecans, chopped
8 ounces cream cheese, softened
1 cup confectioners' sugar
2 cups frozen whipped topping, thawed
1 (3-ounce) package chocolate instant pudding mix
1 (3-ounce) package vanilla instant pudding mix
2 cups milk
3 cups frozen whipped topping, thawed
3 ($1^{1}/_{2}$-ounce) chocolate candy bars, grated

Mix the melted margarine, flour and pecans in a bowl. Press into a 9×13-inch baking pan. Bake at 350 degrees for 20 minutes. Place on a wire rack and let cool completely. Mix the cream cheese, confectioners' sugar and 2 cups whipped topping in a bowl until smooth. Spread over the cooled crust. Combine the chocolate pudding mix, vanilla pudding mix and milk in a bowl. Whisk for 2 minutes or until smooth. Pour over the cream cheese layer. Spread with 3 cups whipped topping and sprinkle with the grated chocolate. Cover and chill until set.

Yield: 15 servings

Banana Pudding

1 (6-ounce) package vanilla instant pudding mix
3 cups frozen whipped topping, thawed
3 cups milk
8 ounces cream cheese, softened
1 (14-ounce) can sweetened condensed milk
1 (14-ounce) box vanilla wafers
7 or 8 bananas, sliced
3 cups frozen whipped topping, thawed

Combine the pudding mix, 3 cups whipped topping, milk, cream cheese and sweetened condensed milk in a large bowl. Beat until smooth. Crumble the vanilla wafers in the bottom of a 9×13-inch baking dish. Arrange the banana slices on top. Pour the pudding mixture over the bananas. Spread with 3 cups whipped topping.

Yield: 15 servings

There were plentiful supplies of flour, fig cakes, raisin cakes, wine, oil, cattle and sheep, for there was joy in Israel.
I Chronicles 12:40

Martha Howard's Brownies

1/2 cup (1 stick) butter
2 ounces semisweet chocolate
1 cup sugar
2 eggs, beaten
2/3 cup flour
1/2 teaspoon vanilla extract
1/2 cup pecans, chopped

Melt the butter and chocolate in a saucepan over low heat. Pour into a bowl. Beat in the sugar and eggs. Add the flour and stir to mix well. Add the vanilla and pecans and stir to mix well. Pour into a greased 9-inch square baking pan. Bake at 325 degrees for 25 minutes. Place on a wire rack to cool. Cut into squares when cool.

Yield: 16 brownies

John answered, "The man with two tunics should share with him who has none, and the one who has food should do the same."
Luke 3:11

Brownie Trifle

1 (19-ounce) package fudge brownie mix
2 eggs
1/2 cup vegetable oil
1 (3-ounce) package chocolate instant pudding mix
3 cups milk
1 (8-ounce) package milk chocolate toffee bits
1 (12-ounce) container frozen whipped topping, thawed
Chocolate curls

Combine the brownie mix, eggs and oil in a large bowl. Mix according to the package directions. Spread in a nonstick 9×13-inch baking pan. Bake according to the package directions. Place on a wire rack to cool. Crumble into pieces when cool.

Combine the pudding mix and milk in a bowl. Whisk for 2 minutes or until smooth. Place half the crumbled brownies in a 3-quart trifle bowl. Top with half the pudding. Sprinkle with half the toffee bits. Top with half the whipped topping. Repeat the layers and top with chocolate curls. Cover and chill for 8 hours.

Yield: 12 servings

Cream Cheese Brownies

Cream Cheese Mixture
2 tablespoons butter, softened
3 ounces cream cheese, softened
1/4 cup sugar
1 egg
1 tablespoon flour
1/2 teaspoon vanilla extract

Brownie Mixture
3 tablespoons butter
4 ounces sweet chocolate
2 eggs
3/4 cup sugar
1/2 cup flour
1/2 teaspoon baking powder
1/4 teaspoon salt
1 teaspoon vanilla extract
1/4 teaspoon almond extract
1/2 cup nuts, chopped

For the cream cheese mixture, beat the butter and cream cheese in a mixing bowl until light and fluffy. Beat in the sugar gradually until fluffy. Add the egg, flour and vanilla and beat until smooth.

For the brownie mixture, melt the butter and chocolate in a saucepan over low heat. Let cool. Beat the eggs in a bowl until thick and pale yellow. Beat in the sugar gradually until thick. Add the flour, baking powder and salt and stir to mix well. Stir in the cooled chocolate. Stir in the vanilla and almond extract. Add the nuts and stir to mix well. Remove 1 cup of the brownie mixture. Pour the remaining brownie mixture into a greased 9-inch square baking dish. Spread the cream cheese mixture evenly on top. Drop the reserved brownie mixture by spoonfuls onto the cream cheese layer. Swirl through the 3 layers gently with a knife. Bake at 350 degrees for 35 to 40 minutes. Place on a wire rack to cool. Cut into squares when cool.

Yield: 16 brownies

Luscious Lemon Squares

Crust

1 cup (2 sticks) butter, softened
1/2 cup confectioners' sugar
2 cups flour

Filling

3 extra-large eggs
2 cups sugar
1/4 cup lemon juice
Grated zest of 1 large lemon
1/4 cup flour
1/2 teaspoon baking powder
Confectioners' sugar for sprinkling

For the crust, mix the butter and confectioners' sugar in a bowl until smooth. Add the flour and stir until blended. Press onto the bottom of a 9×13-inch baking dish. Bake at 350 degrees for 15 minutes or until golden brown. Place on a wire rack to cool.

For the filling, whisk the eggs in a bowl until thick. Whisk in the sugar, lemon juice, lemon zest, flour and baking powder. Pour over the hot crust. Bake at 350 degrees for 25 minutes or until set. Place on a wire rack and let cool slightly. Cut into squares and sprinkle with confectioners' sugar. Let cool completely before removing from the pan.

Yield: 24 squares

Creole Pralines

2 cups sugar
1 cup packed brown sugar
1/2 cup (1 stick) butter
1 cup milk
2 tablespoons light corn syrup
4 cups pecan halves, chopped

Combine the sugar, brown sugar, butter, milk and corn syrup in a 3-quart saucepan. Bring to a boil over high heat, stirring constantly. Reduce the heat to medium. Cook for about 20 minutes or to 234 to 240 degrees on a candy thermometer, soft-ball stage. Remove from the heat and stir in the pecans. Drop by spoonfuls quickly onto waxed paper.

Yield: 40 pralines

Texas Gold Bars

1 (18-ounce) box yellow cake mix
1 egg, beaten
1/2 cup (1 stick) margarine, melted
16 ounces cream cheese, softened
2 eggs, beaten
1 (1-pound) package confectioners' sugar
1 teaspoon vanilla extract
Confectioners' sugar for sprinkling

Combine the cake mix, 1 egg and melted margarine in a bowl. Stir to mix well. Press onto the bottom of a 9×13-inch baking dish. Beat the cream cheese, 2 eggs, 1 package confectioners' sugar and vanilla in a bowl until smooth. Spread over the cake mixture. Bake at 325 degrees for 1 hour. Place on a wire rack and let cool completely. Sprinkle with additional confectioners' sugar and cut into bars.

Yield: 24 bars

Pecan Pie Squares

Crust

$^1/_2$ cup plus 2 tablespoons sugar
$^3/_4$ teaspoon salt
$^3/_4$ cup ($1^1/_2$ sticks) butter, softened
3 cups flour

Filling

4 eggs, beaten
$1^1/_2$ cups sugar
3 tablespoons butter, melted
$1^1/_2$ cups light corn syrup
$1^1/_2$ teaspoons vanilla extract
$2^1/_2$ cups pecans, chopped

For the crust, combine the sugar, salt, butter and flour in a bowl. Beat with an electric mixer until crumbly. Press onto the bottom of a 10×15-inch baking pan. Bake at 350 degrees for 20 minutes. Place on a wire rack.

For the filling, combine the eggs, sugar, melted butter, corn syrup, vanilla and pecans and stir to mix well. Pour over the hot crust. Bake at 350 degrees for 30 minutes or until set. Place on a wire rack and let cool. Cut into squares.

Yield: 35 squares

They gave him water to drink and food to eat—part of a cake of pressed figs and two cakes of raisins. He ate and was revived.
I Samuel 30:11, 12

Favorite Sugar Cookies

Cookies
3/4 cup (1 1/2 sticks) butter, softened
1/2 cup packed brown sugar
1 tablespoon sugar
1 egg yolk
1 teaspoon vanilla extract
2 cups sifted flour

Frosting
1/2 cup (1 stick) butter, softened
1 (1-pound) package confectioners' sugar
3 tablespoons milk
1 teaspoon vanilla extract
Few drops of food coloring (optional)

For the cookies, cream the butter, brown sugar and sugar in a mixing bowl until light and fluffy. Add the egg and vanilla and beat well. Stir in the flour. Shape into balls using 1 to 2 teaspoonfuls of dough for each ball. Place on greased cookie sheets. Flatten each ball with the bottom of a glass. Bake at 350 degrees for 7 to 9 minutes. Remove the cookies to a wire rack to cool.

For the frosting, beat the butter, confectioners' sugar, milk and vanilla in a bowl until smooth. Beat in the food coloring. Spread the frosting on the cooled cookies.

Yield: 2 dozen cookies

Note: If you do not wish to frost the cookies, dip the bottom of the glass into sugar before pressing on the cookie dough.

Frosted Christmas Cookies

Cookies
1 cup (2 sticks) butter, softened
$1^3/4$ cups confectioners' sugar
1 egg, beaten
2 teaspoons vanilla extract
Grated zest of 1 lemon
2 tablespoons lemon juice
$2^1/2$ cups flour
1 teaspoon baking soda
$^1/4$ teaspoon salt

Frosting
$2^1/2$ cups confectioners' sugar
$^1/4$ teaspoon cream of tartar
2 egg whites
Red and green food coloring

For the cookies, cream the butter and confectioners' sugar in a mixing bowl until light and fluffy. Beat in the egg, vanilla, lemon zest and lemon juice. Add the flour, baking soda and salt. Stir to mix well. Divide the dough into halves and wrap each half in plastic wrap. Chill for several hours or until firm. Roll out 1 ball of dough to $^1/4$ inch thick on a floured work surface. Cut into desired shapes with cookie cutters. Place on ungreased cookie sheets. Repeat with the remaining ball of dough. Bake the cookies at 325 degrees for 12 to 15 minutes or until light brown. Remove the cookies to a wire rack to cool.

For the frosting, beat the confectioners' sugar, cream of tartar and egg whites in a bowl until slightly thickened. Remove half the frosting to a bowl and add red food coloring to achieve the desired shade. Add green food coloring to the remaining frosting to achieve the desired shade. Spread the frosting on the cooled cookies.

Yield: 4 dozen cookies

Crispy Oat Cookies

1 cup (2 sticks) butter, softened
1 cup sugar
1 cup packed brown sugar
1 egg
1 cup vegetable oil
1 teaspoon vanilla extract
$3^1/_2$ cups flour
1 teaspoon baking soda
$^1/_2$ teaspoon salt
1 cup rolled oats
1 cup cornflakes, crushed
$^1/_2$ cup flaked coconut
$^1/_2$ cup pecans, chopped

Cream the butter in a large mixing bowl until light and fluffy. Beat in the sugar and brown sugar until blended. Beat in the egg. Add the oil and vanilla and beat to mix well. Mix the flour, baking soda and salt in a bowl. Add to the butter mixture and stir to mix well. Stir in the oats, cornflakes, coconut and pecans. Shape into 1-inch balls and place on ungreased cookie sheets. Flatten with a fork. Bake at 325 degrees for 15 minutes. Remove the cookies to a wire rack to cool.

Yield: 10 dozen cookies

Mabel Anne Muhm's Oatmeal Chocolate Chip Cookies

1 cup shortening
1 cup packed brown sugar
2 eggs, beaten
2 teaspoons vanilla extract
1½ cups flour
1 teaspoon baking soda
½ teaspoon salt
2 cups rolled oats
1 cup pecans, chopped
1 cup semisweet chocolate chips

Beat the shortening and brown sugar in a mixing bowl until light and fluffy. Beat in the eggs and vanilla. Stir in the flour, baking soda and salt. Add the oats, pecans and chocolate chips and stir to mix well. Drop by spoonfuls onto greased cookie sheets. Bake at 350 degrees for 15 minutes. Remove the cookies to a wire rack to cool.

Yield: 2 dozen cookies

Snickerdoodles

1 cup shortening
1 1/2 cups sugar
2 eggs, beaten
1/2 teaspoon vanilla extract
2 3/4 cups flour
1 teaspoon cream of tartar
1 teaspoon baking soda
1 teaspoon salt
2 teaspoons cinnamon
2 tablespoons sugar

Cream the shortening and 1 1/2 cups sugar in a mixing bowl until light and fluffy. Add the eggs 1 at a time, beating well after each addition. Stir in the vanilla. Sift the flour, cream of tartar, baking soda and salt into a bowl. Add to the shortening mixture and stir to mix well. Form the dough into small balls. Mix the cinnamon and 2 tablespoons sugar in a shallow dish. Roll the balls in the cinnamon mixture. Place 2 inches apart on ungreased cookie sheets. Bake at 400 degrees for 8 to 10 minutes. Remove the cookies to a wire rack to cool.

Yield: 4 dozen cookies

Grammy's Wedding Cookies

1 cup (2 sticks) butter, softened
1/4 cup sugar
2 teaspoons vanilla extract
2 cups flour
Dash of salt
2 cups pecans, finely chopped
Sifted confectioners' sugar

Cream the butter and sugar in a mixing bowl until light and fluffy. Stir in the vanilla. Mix the flour and salt in a bowl. Stir gradually into the butter mixture. Stir in the pecans; the dough will be stiff. Form the dough into balls the size of small walnuts. Place on ungreased cookie sheets. Bake at 350 degrees for 22 to 25 minutes. Roll the hot cookies in confectioners' sugar and place on a wire rack to cool. Roll again in confectioners' sugar when cool.

Yield: 4 dozen cookies

Chocolate Crinkles

2 cups sugar
$^1/_2$ cup vegetable oil
2 teaspoons vanilla extract
4 ounces unsweetened chocolate, melted and cooled
4 eggs, beaten
2 cups flour
2 teaspoons baking powder
$^1/_2$ teaspoon salt
1 cup confectioners' sugar

Mix the sugar, oil, vanilla and melted chocolate in a large bowl. Add the eggs 1 at a time, stirring well after each addition. Stir in the flour, baking powder and salt and mix well. Cover and chill for at least 3 hours. Drop the dough by teaspoonfuls into the confectioners' sugar in a bowl. Roll to coat the dough. Shape into balls. Place 2 inches apart on greased cookie sheets. Bake at 350 degrees for 10 to 12 minutes or until almost no indentation remains when touched in the center. Remove the cookies to a wire rack to cool.

Yield: 6 dozen cookies

Mud Dobbers

4 ounces unsweetened chocolate
12 ounces semisweet chocolate
3/4 cup (1 1/2 sticks) unsalted butter
4 eggs
1 1/2 cups sugar
4 teaspoons instant coffee powder
4 teaspoons vanilla extract
1/2 cup unbleached flour
1/2 teaspoon baking powder
1 teaspoon salt
2 cups semisweet chocolate chips
4 cups walnuts, broken into large pieces

Place the unsweetened chocolate, semisweet chocolate and butter in the top of a double boiler. Cook over simmering water until melted. Cover and cook for a few minutes longer. Remove from the heat and stir. Let cool slightly. Combine the eggs, sugar, coffee powder and vanilla in a large bowl. Beat at high speed with an electric mixer for 1 to 2 minutes. Add the melted chocolate mixture and beat at low speed just until mixed. Sift the flour, baking powder and salt into a bowl. Add to the chocolate mixture and beat just until mixed. Stir in the chocolate chips and walnuts. Chill for 2 to 3 hours. Scoop 1/3 cup of the dough for each cookie and place 2 inches apart on greased cookie sheets. Bake at 350 degrees for no longer than 16 to 17 minutes. Remove the cookies to a wire rack to cool.

Yield: 2 dozen cookies

Index

For Such a Time as This
A Cookbook

Park Cities Baptist Church
3933 Northwest Parkway
Dallas, Texas 75225
214-860-1563

Your Order	Qty	Total
For Such a Time as This: A Cookbook at $20.00 per book		$
Postage and handling at $4.00 per book		$
	Total	$

Please make check payable to Park Cities Baptist Church—Capital Campaign.

Name

Address

City State Zip

Telephone Email

Photocopies will be accepted.